Student's Test Booklet

Neue Freunde

 **HARCOURT BRACE JOVANOVICH, PUBLISHERS**

Orlando   San Diego   Chicago   Dallas

Writer   **Margrit Diehl**

Editorial Advisor   **Charles R. Hancock**
Ohio State University
Columbus, OH

Contributors   **Fred Schneider**
Eleanor Roosevelt High School
Greenbelt, MD

Renate Vendel
Walter Johnson High School
Bethesda, MD

Art: PC&F, Inc.

Printed in the United States of America
ISBN 0-15-383508-7

CONTENTS

Quizzes

Tests

Proficiency-Based Tests

QUIZ 1 Unit 1 • Section A

Maximum Score: 20 points

A. You will hear six greetings or goodbyes. For each one, decide whether the response you hear is appropriate or not. Place a check mark in the appropriate row.
6 points

	1	2	3	4	5	6
appropriate						
not appropriate						

SCORE ☐

B. Some people are greeting each other or saying goodbye. Read what each one says and circle the letter of the appropriate response.
6 points

1. Grüss dich, Christof!

   a. Morgen, Michael!

   b. Wiedersehen, Michael!

   c. Tschüs!

2. Guten Morgen, Frau Binder!

   a. Auf Wiedersehen, Monika!

   b. Tag, Monika!

   c. Bis dann!

3. Wiedersehen, Jörg!

   a. Hallo, Claudia!

   b. Guten Tag!

   c. Tschau, Claudia!

4. Tschüs, Andreas! Bis dann!

   a. Tschau!

   b. Grüss dich!

   c. Guten Morgen!

5. Tag, Ulrike!

   a. Grüss dich, Stefan!

   b. Tschüs, Stefan!

   c. Wiedersehen, Stefan!

6. Auf Wiedersehen, Herr Sperling!

   a. Tag!

   b. Hallo!

   c. Wiedersehen!

SCORE ☐

C. How would you greet and say goodbye to the following people? What would they say to you in response? Write four exchanges.
8 points

1. one of your classmates

_____

_____

_____

_____

2. your German teacher

_____

_____

_____

_____

SCORE ☐

QUIZ 2   Unit 1 • Section B

Maximum Score: 22 points

A. You will hear four short conversations. Each conversation refers to one of the pictures below. Write the number of the conversation under the corresponding picture.
4 points

____   ____   ____   ____

SCORE [   ]

B. Some students are asking the names of new classmates. Read the conversations and fill in the missing words.
10 points

A: Wie _____ du?
    (1)

B: Ich _____ Andreas.
    (2)

A: _____ heisst _____ Junge?
    (3)   (4)

B: Er _____ Peter.
    (5)

A: _____ ist das?
    (6)

B: Das _____ Herr Sperling.
    (7)

A: Wie _____ _____ Mädchen?
    (8)   (9)

B: Sie _____ Kirsten.
    (10)

SCORE [   ]

C. Write two dialogs. (1) In the first, you introduce yourself to a new student. Greet him, give him your name, and ask him his. (2) In the second, you are talking to a friend. You see a teacher you don't know and ask the friend who it is. Your friend tells you it's the German teacher. You ask her name and the friend tells you her name is Braun. Use complete sentences.

8 points

1. A: _____

   B: _____

   A: _____

   B: _____

2. A: _____

   B: _____

   A: _____

   B: _____

SCORE ☐

QUIZ 3   Unit 1 • Section C

Maximum Score: 20 points

A. Listen carefully to each sequence of numbers. For each one, write the number that should come next. Use numerals, not words.
8 points

1. _____   3. _____   5. _____   7. _____

2. _____   4. _____   6. _____   8. _____

SCORE [   ]

B. Two young people are talking about their ages and the ages of their friends. Complete the dialog by filling in each blank with the correct form of **sein**.
8 points

A: Petra, wie alt _____ du?
(1)

B: Ich _____ dreizehn.
(2)

A: Wie alt _____ Sabine?
(3)

B: Sie _____ auch dreizehn.
(4)

A: Und der Paul? Wie alt _____ er?
(5)

B: Paul _____ fünfzehn.
(6)

A: Und Steffi und Jörg? Wie alt _____ sie?
(7)

B: Sie _____ vierzehn.
(8)

SCORE [   ]

C. Write two sentences about each of the students pictured.
4 points

Stefan, 15

Antje, 16

1. a. _____

  b. _____

2. a. _____

  b. _____

SCORE [ ]

QUIZ 4   Unit 1 • Section D

Maximum Score: 20 points

A. Listen to the following questions and answers. For each set, decide whether the response is appropriate to the question or not. Place a check mark in the appropriate row.
6 points

	1	2	3	4	5	6
appropriate						
not appropriate						

SCORE

B. You meet a new teacher. Write three questions; ask (1) if she is the German teacher, (2) what her name is, and (3) where she is from.
3 points

1. _____

2. _____

3. _____

SCORE

C. Suppose you didn't understand the information crossed out in each statement. What question would you ask? Write the questions.
5 points

1. Er heisst ~~Hans-Jochen.~~   _____

2. Ich bin aus ~~Buxtehude.~~   _____

3. Der Junge ist ~~14 Jahre alt.~~   _____

4. ~~Der Deutschlehrer heisst~~

   ~~Herr Neustiefelmeier.~~   _____

5. Das ist die ~~Hannelore.~~   _____

SCORE

D. Look at the map and write three sentences about each boy and girl pictured. Give the name, age, and country of each one.
6 points

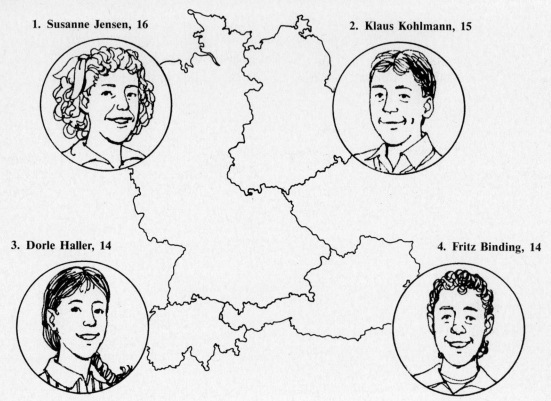

1. Susanne Jensen, 16

2. Klaus Kohlmann, 15

3. Dorle Haller, 14

4. Fritz Binding, 14

1. a. _____

   b. _____

   c. _____

2. a. _____

   b. _____

   c. _____

3. a. _____

   b. _____

   c. _____

4. a. _____

   b. _____

   c. _____

SCORE ☐

QUIZ 5   Unit 2 • Section A

Maximum Score: 24 points

A. You will hear how various students and teachers get to school. Write the number of the sentence you hear under the corresponding picture.
6 points

_____   _____   _____   _____   _____   _____

SCORE [ ]

B. Two friends are talking about how their friends and teachers get to school. Complete the dialog by filling in each blank with the correct form of **kommen** or the method of getting to school, using the pictures as cues.
15 points

A: Wie _____ du in die Schule?
 (1)

B: Ich _____ mit dem 🚲 _____ .
 (2)   (3)

A: _____ Ulrike auch mit dem 🚲 _____ ?
 (4)   (5)

B: Nein, sie _____ mit dem 🚌 _____ .
 (6)   (7)

A: Herr Frisch und Herr Sahler _____ mit dem 🚗 _____ .
 (8)   (9)

B: Frau Siebert _____ 👢 _____ .
 (10)   (11)

A: Schau, da _____ Jens mit dem 🛵 _____ !
 (12)   (13)

B: Und da _____ Margit mit der 🚋 _____ .
 (14)   (15)

SCORE [ ]

C. How do you and your friends get to school? Write three sentences, one about yourself and one each about two of your friends.
3 points

1. _____

2. _____

3. _____

SCORE [   ]

QUIZ 6 Unit 2 • Section B

Maximum Score: 25 points

A. You will hear a conversation that takes place in a stationery store that sells school supplies. Write the number of each statement or question under the corresponding picture.
4½ points

_____ _____ _____ _____ _____

_____ _____ _____ _____

SCORE [ ]

B. Complete the following dialog by filling in each blank with the correct article or pronoun.
8 points

A: Du, Monika, wo ist _____ Wörterbuch?
(1)

B: _____ ist dort drüben.
(2)

A: Ist _____ Taschenrechner auch dort drüben?
(3)

B: Nein, _____ ist weg.
(4)

A: Unsinn! Schau mal!

B: Und _____ Kassetten? Wo sind _____?
(5) (6)

A: Hier.

B: Wo ist _____ Schultasche?
(7)

A: Ich weiss nicht. Ist _____ nicht da?
(8)

SCORE [ ]

C. Write a dialog that takes place in a store. You are the customer and want to know the price of the pocket calculator and the ballpoint pens. Don't forget to be polite.
5 points

DU _____
(1)

VERKÄUFERIN _____
(2)

DU _____
(3)

VERKÄUFERIN _____
(4)

DU _____
(5)

VERKÄUFERIN _____
(6)

DM 18,00

DM 4,00

SCORE ☐

D. For each of the following nouns, write the singular definite article in the first blank and the plural definite article along with the plural in the second and third blanks.
7½ points

1. _____ Bleistift, _____ _____

2. _____ Lehrer, _____ _____

3. _____ Schultasche, _____ _____

4. _____ Mädchen, _____ _____

5. _____ Heft, _____ _____

6. _____ Junge, _____ _____

7. _____ Stundenplan, _____ _____

8. _____ Lehrerin, _____ _____

9. _____ Buch, _____ _____

10. _____ Kuli, _____ _____

SCORE ☐

QUIZ 7   Unit 2 • Section C

Maximum Score: 21 points

A. Fill in the class schedule below according to what you hear. Write the name of the subject in the appropriate slot. You will hear each item twice.
5 points

Stundenplan für *Jens Kröger 92*					
Zeit	Montag	Dienstag	Mittwoch	Donnerstag	Freitag	Samstag
8.00 – 8.40		Deutsch	Mathe	—	Physik	
8.45 – 9.30	Deutsch	Mathe	Deutsch	Physik		
9.30 – 9.45	—		Pause			
9.45 – 10.30	Religion	Englisch	Englisch		Deutsch	
10.30 – 11.15	Biologie			Englisch	Latein	
11.15 – 11.30	—		Pause			
11.30 – 12.15	Latein	Geschichte	Sport	Geschichte	Kunst	
12.15 – 13.00	Musik	—	Sport	Geographie		

SCORE _____

B. Write each of the times shown on these digital clocks in two ways. Spell out the numbers.
8 points

1. `2:15` _____
    _____

2. `6:45` _____
    _____

3. `9:50` _____
    _____

4. `8:30` _____
    _____

SCORE _____

C. Complete the following dialog by filling in each blank with the correct form of **haben**.
8 points

FRANK   Was _____ du jetzt? Biologie?
                      (1)

MICHAEL Nein, ich _____ Mathe. Klaus und Marianne _____
                        (2)   (3)

          Biologie.

FRANK   Paul _____ jetzt Englisch. Kirsten und Monika, _____
                    (4)   (5)

          ihr auch Englisch?

MONIKA   Ja, wir _____ auch Englisch.
                      (6)

KIRSTEN Was _____ Sabine jetzt?
                      (7)

FRANK   Sie _____ jetzt Deutsch.
                   (8)

SCORE [ ]

QUIZ 8 Unit 2 • Section D

Maximum Score: 20 points

A. Some students are talking about their grades. For each statement, decide whether the response is appropriate or not. Place a check mark in the appropriate row.
5 points

	1	2	3	4	5
appropriate					
not appropriate					

SCORE _____

B. Write an appropriate response to each of the following statements or questions.
8 points

1. Ich habe eine Eins in Mathe. _____

2. Ist Deutsch schwer? _____

3. Was hast du in Englisch? _____

4. Paul hat eine Fünf in Latein. _____

5. Geographie ist leicht. _____

6. Ich habe eine Zwei in Biologie. _____

7. Biologie ist toll! _____

8. Eine Drei in Physik ist nicht schlecht. _____

SCORE _____

C. The following two dialog are incompete. Supply appropriate sentences to complete them.
7 points

A: _____
   (1)

B: Nein, Algebra ist nicht schwer.

A: _____
   (2)

B: Ich habe eine Eins.

A: _____
   (3)

B: Ja, das ist gut.

A: Carola hat eine Zwei in Mathe.

B: _____
   (4)

A: Was hat sie in Chemie?

B: _____
   (5)

A: Schade! Sind die Hausaufgaben und Klassenarbeiten in Chemie schwer?

B: _____
   (6)

A: Und in Bio? Sind sie auch so schwer?

B: _____
   (7)

SCORE ☐

QUIZ 9   Unit 3 • Section A

Maximum Score: 21 points

A. What do these young people do in their free time? Write the number of the sentence in which you hear a sport or hobby mentioned under the picture of that sport or hobby.
8 points

_____   _____   _____   _____

_____   _____   _____   _____

SCORE [   ]

B. You are asking various people about their interests. Read the incomplete questions below and decide which of the choices in the box best completes each one. Fill in the blanks with the names of the people you are addressing.
3 points

Herr Siebert — Karin — Jens und Jörg

1. _____, macht ihr Sport?

2. _____, sammelst du Briefmarken?

3. _____, spielen Sie ein Instrument?

SCORE [   ]

C. Some girls and boys are playing cards. Complete the paragraph by filling in each blank with the correct form of an appropriate verb. Use the verbs in the box.
4 points

| gewinnen — heissen — mogeln — spielen |

Die Mädchen und Jungen _____ Karten. Das Spiel _____
(1)   (2)

Mau-Mau. Karin _____ , aber Hans ist sauer. „Du _____ ! "
(3)   (4)

sagt Hans.

SCORE [   ]

D. You are asking a classmate about his or her interests. Write three questions and an appropriate answer for each one.
6 points

1. a. _____

   b. _____

2. a. _____

   b. _____

3. a. _____

   b. _____

SCORE [   ]

QUIZ 10   Unit 3 • Section B

Maximum Score: 26 points

A. Lydia is talking about the sports she does at different times of the year. Listen to what she says and place a check mark in each of the appropriate boxes.
7 points

	Fussball	Basketball	Schwimmen	Schilaufen	Segeln	Tennis
Frühjahr						
Sommer						
Herbst						
Winter						

SCORE _____

B. Read the following paragraph about Helmut and then read the incomplete statements below. Decide which of the lettered choices correctly completes each statement according to the information in the paragraph. Circle that letter.
4 points

Helmut spielt am Dienstag und Donnerstag Basketball.
Am Samstag und Sonntag spielt er Fussball. Er spielt nur
einmal im Jahr Tennis. Hockey spielt er nicht.

1. Helmut spielt _____ Basketball.

   a. nie

   b. einmal im Monat

   c. zweimal in der Woche

2. Er spielt _____ Fussball.

   a. am Wochenende

   b. dreimal in der Woche

   c. zweimal in Monat

3. Er spielt _____ Tennis.

   a. manchmal

   b. oft

   c. selten

4. Er spielt _____ Hockey.

   a. einmal im Jahr

   b. nie

   c. meistens

SCORE _____

C. You have to report on when and how often Uwe participates in sports. He has jotted down some notes for you. Referring to the notes, write the report. Use the **er-**form.
6 points

```
    Sommer  —  meistens Schwimmen
    Winter  —  oft Volleyball, manchmal Eishockey
Frühjahr  —  Tennis, dreimal in der Woche
                 Basketball, einmal in der Woche
    Herbst  —  immer Fussball
```

SCORE [   ]

D. Fill in this chart for yourself. Write at least one sport or activity in each column. Then write a paragraph about yourself, telling what sports and activities you do and how often you do them.
9 points

nie	selten	manchmal	oft	meistens	immer

SCORE [   ]

QUIZ 11 Unit 3 • Section C

Maximum Score: 22 points

A. You will hear some young people say what they like to do in their free time. Listen to what each one says and write down the sports and activities each one likes.
4 points

1. _____

2. _____

3. _____

4. _____

SCORE [   ]

B. A student is being interviewed about his hobbies and interests. The questions and answers got mixed up. Read the interview and number the questions and answers in a logical sequence.
8 points

_____ Am liebsten höre ich Rockmusik. Aber Jazz ist auch nicht schlecht.

_____ Ja, ich sammle Musikkassetten.

_____ Wie findest du Fussball?

_____ Was machst du in deiner Freizeit?

_____ Toll! Ich spiele oft.

_____ Wirklich? Hörst du gern Rockmusik, oder hörst du lieber Jazz?

_____ Und hast du auch Hobbys?

_____ Ich spiele Fussball.

SCORE [   ]

C. Do you agree or disagree with the following statements? Write what you would say.
6 points

1. Faulenzen ist super! _____

2. Schach ist interessant. _____

3. Ich finde Kartenspielen langweilig. _____

4. Gymnastik ist schwer. _____

5. Sammeln ist blöd. _____

6. Fussball ist Spitze! _____

SCORE [   ]

D. Write a paragraph about your own likes and dislikes. Write what you like to do, what
you prefer, and what you like most of all. Mention also what you don't like.
4 points

_____

_____

_____

_____

_____

SCORE [   ]

QUIZ 12   Unit 5 • Section A

Maximum Score: 22 points

A. Peter gets everything ready for his trip and finally gets on the plane. Listen to the fragments of conversation between Peter and his father and between Peter and a young traveler he meets on the plane. For each conversation fragment, determine whether the second person's response is appropriate or not. Place a check mark in the appropriate row.
5 points

	1	2	3	4	5
appropriate					
not appropriate					

SCORE ☐

B. Read the following incomplete sentences about Peter and decide which of the lettered answer choices correctly completes each one. Write the letter in the space provided.
5 points

_____ 1. Peter fliegt morgen   a. den Vati.

_____ 2. In Deutschland besucht er   b. die Reiseschecks?

_____ 3. Er bleibt   c. Freunde, die Familie Nedel in Neuss.

_____ 4. Moment mal! Wo sind   d. nach Deutschland.

_____ 5. Ich frage mal   e. vier Wochen.

SCORE ☐

C. Peter and his father are checking if Peter has everything for the trip. Using the pictures as cues, complete what Herr Seber says and how Peter responds.
12 points

HERR SEBER   Hast du...?   PETER   Ja, hier ist (sind)...

1. _____   _____

2. _____   _____

3. _____   _____

4. _____   _____

5. _____   _____

6. _____   _____

7. _____   _____

8. _____   _____

9. _____   _____

10. _____   _____

11. _____   _____

12. _____   _____

SCORE

QUIZ 13   Unit 5 • Section B

Maximum Score: 22 points

A. Peter is at the airport, questioning the clerk at the information desk. Are the information clerk's responses appropriate or not? Place a check mark in the appropriate row.
5 points

	1	2	3	4	5
appropriate					
not appropriate					

SCORE

B. Read the paragraph about Peter's arrival in Frankfurt. Then read the statements below and determine whether each one is true or false. Place a check mark in the appropriate row.
6 points

Peter fliegt nach Deutschland. Das Flugzeug landet in Frankfurt. Peter geht durch die Passkontrolle, holt das Gepäck und geht durch den Zoll. Er hat nichts zu verzollen und geht bei Grün durch. Er hat Zeit und möchte etwas essen. Er geht zur Auskunft und fragt: „Wo ist bitte das Restaurant?" − „Dort drüben, links." Er geht ins Restaurant, bestellt etwas zu essen und liest den Reiseführer. Aber Moment mal! Er braucht Geld! Wo ist die Bank? Er muss Geld wechseln, dann kann er essen!

	stimmt	stimmt nicht
1. Frankfurt ist in Deutschland.		
2. Peter hat etwas zu verzollen und geht bei Rot durch.		
3. Er geht zur Auskunft und wechselt dort Geld.		
4. Die Frau an der Auskunft sagt: „Den Pass, bitte!"		
5. Im Restaurant möchte Peter etwas essen.		
6. Aber er kann nicht essen. Er muss Geld wechseln.		

SCORE

C. You are asking for directions in the airport. Complete each statement by filling in the blank with an appropriate verb from the boxed list. You may use a verb more than once.
6 points

> essen — fragen — kaufen — telefonieren — wechseln

1. Wo ist bitte die Bank? Ich möchte Geld _____.

2. Wo ist die Auskunft? Ich möchte etwas _____.

3. Wo ist das Restaurant? Ich möchte etwas _____.

4. Wo ist der Geschenkladen? Ich möchte ein Geschenk _____.

5. Wo ist die Post? Ich möchte Briefmarken _____.

6. Wo ist das Telefon? Ich möchte _____.

SCORE ☐

D. As you wait for your flight to Frankfurt, you fall into conversation with a fellow student. Complete the dialog by supplying your new friend's questions.
5 points

STUDENT _____
(1)

DU Ich fliege nach Deutschland.

STUDENT _____
(2)

DU Ich besuche Freunde in München.

STUDENT _____
(3)

DU Von Frankfurt nach München? Mit dem Auto.

STUDENT _____
(4)

DU Hm, so ungefähr 400 Kilometer.

STUDENT _____
(5)

DU Ja, wo ist ein Restaurant?

SCORE ☐

QUIZ 14 Unit 5 • Section C

Maximum Score: 26 points

A. You will hear some announcements of flight departure times at the airport. Look at the monitor as you listen to the announcements. Write the number of the announcement next to the corresponding information on the monitor.
5 points

Flug		nach	um	Gate
LH	204	New York	14^{45}	D
LH	626	Paris	16^{50}	B
LH	412	Hamburg	13^{00}	B
LH	174	London	20^{30}	A
LH	300	Tokio	18^{20}	C

_____
_____
_____
_____
_____

SCORE [ ]

B. Peter Seber is calling Frau Nedel from the airport. Put their phone conversation into the correct order. Number the sentences in a logical sequence.
9 points

_____ Ach so! Und wann bist du in Köln?

_____ Grüss dich, Peter! Wo bist du?

_____ Hier Nedel.

_____ Ich bin in Frankfurt.

_____ Ja, hier Peter Seber.

_____ Prima! Auf Wiederhören, Frau Nedel!

_____ Um 13 Uhr. Flug LH 368.

_____ Um 13 Uhr? Schön, wir sind pünktlich da.

_____ Wiederhören, Peter!

SCORE [ ]

C. Peter is at the bank, changing money. Complete the dialog by filling in the blanks with the missing words.
7 points

PETER   Ich möchte 50 Dollar _____.
                                                                    (1)

BANKANGESTELLTER   In D-Mark?

PETER   Ja, _____.
                                              (2)

BANKANGESTELLTER   Der _____ ist heute DM 2,34.
                                              (3)

PETER   Hm, das ist nicht _____.
                                                                (4)

BANKANGESTELLTER   So, 50 Dollar. Das _____ 117 Mark.
                                                                (5)

PETER   _____!
                                              (6)

BANKANGESTELLTER   Bitte! Und schöne _____!
                                                                (7)

SCORE ⬚

D. You have just arrived in Germany and want to make a phone call. Here's what you do. Complete the paragraph by filling in each blank with the correct form of an appropriate verb from the boxed list.
5 points

| gehen — heben — stecken — wählen — wechseln |

Du _____ Geld, du _____
            (1)   (2)

in eine Telefonzelle, du _____ den Hörer ab, du
                                              (3)

_____ Münzen in den Apparat, und du
            (4)

_____ die Nummer.
            (5)

SCORE ⬚

QUIZ 15   Unit 6 • Section A

Maximum Score: 31 points

A. Sabine is introducing her family. Under the appropriate picture on her family tree, write the name of the person she introduces. You will hear each introduction twice.
10 points

Sabine

SCORE _____

B. Read the following fragments of conversation. Decide whether the second speaker's response is logical or not. Write **ja** or **nein** in the space provided.
5 points

_____ 1. A: Ich habe zwei Geschwister.

           B: Ich habe drei, zwei Brüder und eine Schwester.

_____ 2. A: Das sind meine Grosseltern.

           B: Meine Mutter spielt gut Tennis, und mein Vater sammelt gern Briefmarken.

_____ 3. A: Und hier sind meine Eltern.

           B: Tag, Fritz!

(continued on next page)

_____ 4. A: Onkel Jürgen und Tante Christa kommen aus Berlin.

            B: Sind das die Eltern von deiner Kusine Ali?

_____ 5. A: Das sind zwei Klassenkameraden.

            B: Gehen sie auch in die 9a?

C. A friend of yours is telling you about her family. Complete the paragraph by filling in the blanks with the missing indefinite articles.
10 points

Ich habe _____ Vater und _____ Mutter, _____
             (1)   **(2)**   **(3)**

Schwester und _____ Bruder. Wir haben auch _____ Hund.
                (4)   **(5)**

Ich habe _____ Tante in Kalifornien. Ich habe auch _____
             (6)   **(7)**

Tante und _____ Onkel in New York. Sie haben zwei Kinder,
             (8)

_____ Mädchen und _____ Jungen.
     (9)   **(10)**

D. Pretend you are having a party. Some of your friends and classmates are there. Introduce three members of your family to them. You can include grandparents, aunts, uncles, and cousins. Use the names of your own family members or make up names.
3 points

1. _____

2. _____

3. _____

E. Now three of your friends and classmates introduce themselves to your parents. Write what they say.
3 points

1. _____

2. _____

3. _____

QUIZ 16   Unit 6 • Section B

Maximum Score: 33 points

A. Look at the sketch of the house below as you listen to the descriptions of the rooms. Write the letter of the room or rooms in the space provided next to the number of the description.
5 points

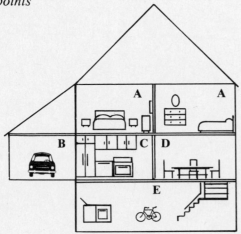

_____ 1.

_____ 2.

_____ 3.

_____ 4.

_____ 5.

SCORE [   ]

B. Read the following exchanges that take place at the Nedels' after Peter arrives. In each case, decide whether the second speaker's response is appropriate or not and write **ja** or **nein** in the space provided.
5 points

_____ 1. A: Das Wohnzimmer sieht so gemütlich aus!

        B: Findest du?

_____ 2. A: Hier ist das Gästezimmer. Das ist jetzt dein Zimmer.

        B: Wie schön!

_____ 3. A: Wir haben auch einen Keller. Prima für eine Party.

        B: Ja, wirklich? Nichts zu danken!

_____ 4. A: Wo sind die Geschenke? Ja, hier, für die Ulrike habe ich ein Buch.

        B: Klein, aber sehr gemütlich.

_____ 5. A: Eine Musikkassette! Mensch, das ist toll! Vielen Dank!

        B: Bitte schön!

SCORE [   ]

C. Write the names of seven rooms in the spaces provided next to this floor plan—any rooms you choose. Then pretend it is your house and write a paragraph telling what rooms you have.
14 points

1. _____

2. _____

3. _____

4. _____

5. _____

6. _____

7. _____

Wir haben _____

_____

_____

D. You are visiting friends and have brought presents. You have brought a calculator for Thomas, a necklace for Barbara, and a book for Frau Müller. Write what you say, how they thank you, and how you respond.
9 points

Du   Ich habe _____ für _____ .
                        (1a)   (1b)

Thomas   _____ .
                            (2)

Du   _____ .
                            (3)

Du   Ich habe _____ für _____ .
                        (4a)   (4b)

Barbara   _____ .
                            (5)

Du   _____ .
                            (6)

Du   Ich habe _____ für _____ .
                        (7a)   (7b)

Frau Müller _____ .
                            (8)

Du   _____ .
                            (9)

QUIZ 17 Unit 6 • Section C

Maximum Score: 22 points

A. These young people are talking about some of their friends and classmates. Listen to the exchanges and, for each one, decide whether the second speaker agrees with the first or not. Place a check mark in the appropriate row.
5 points

	1	2	3	4	5
agree					
disagree					

SCORE

B. Read the descriptions and match them to the pictures. Write the number of the description under the appropriate picture.
5 points

____   ____   ____   ____   ____

1. Es ist klein und gemütlich und hat auch einen hübschen Garten.

2. Sie sind nett und freundlich. Ich finde sie auch sehr lustig. Ich besuche sie oft, und es ist nie langweilig!

3. Sie ist nett, hübsch, brünett. Sie ist auch sehr sportlich. Sie spielt Tennis am liebsten.

4. Er ist gross und schlank, und er hat eine Brille.

5. Sie ist klein aber sehr modern.

SCORE

C. Make up answers to the following questions, using a pronoun. Begin each answer with **ich finde.**
6 points

1. Wie findest du die Antje? Ich finde _____

2. Wie findest du die Schule? _____

3. Wie findest du den Mathelehrer? _____

4. Wie findest du die Klassenkameraden? _____

5. Wie findest du den Garten? _____

6. Wie findest du die Kassetten? _____

SCORE [   ]

D. Describe two people you know, telling how they look, what they like to do, and what you think of them. Write complete sentences.
6 points

_____

_____

_____

_____

_____

_____

SCORE [   ]

QUIZ 18   Unit 7 • Section A

Maximum Score: 20 points

A. You will hear a number of statements about the city of Munich. Look at the street map as you listen to the statements. Decide whether the statements are true or false. Place a check mark in the appropriate row.
5 points

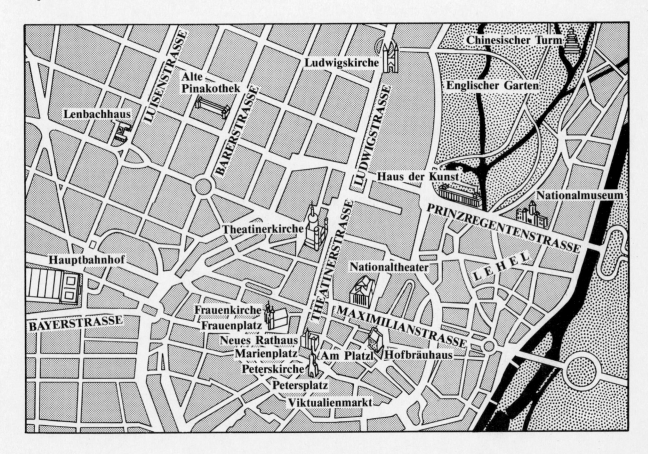

	1	2	3	4	5
stimmt					
stimmt nicht					

SCORE [   ]

B. Choose the most logical answer to each question from the column on the right. In the space provided, write the letter of the answer you choose.
7 points

_____ 1. Wo wohnt Steffi Huber?

_____ 2. Wie gross ist die Stadt München?

_____ 3. Wo ist das Glockenspiel?

_____ 4. Wie heisst die Peterskirche?

_____ 5. Was ist das offizielle Wappen von München?

_____ 6. Wie heisst ein Museum in München?

_____ 7. Wo findest du den Chinesischen Turm?

a. Das Münchner Kindl.

b. Der Alte Peter.

c. Die Alte Pinakothek.

d. Im Englischen Garten.

e. Im Neuen Rathaus am Marienplatz.

f. Sie hat 1,3 Millionen Einwohner.

g. Sie ist in München zu Hause.

SCORE ☐

C. You are in Munich, asking directions to the **Ludwigskirche.** You ask a student your own age, who doesn't know. Then you ask a policeman, who tells you it's in the **Ludwigstrasse.** Write the dialogs.
4 points

Du _____
(1)

Schüler _____
(2)

Du _____
(3)

Polizist _____
(4)

SCORE ☐

D. Write a few sentences about yourself. Introduce yourself, tell where you live, and give some information about that place—for example, whether it is a town or a city, what state it is in, and, perhaps, how many inhabitants it has.
4 points

_____

_____

_____

_____

SCORE ☐

QUIZ 19   Unit 7 • Section B

Maximum Score: 27 points

A. Steffi is going shopping for her mother. Listen to what Frau Huber tells her; then write the number of the sentence under the picture of the item that most appropriately completes the sentence.
10 points

_____   _____   _____   _____

_____   _____   _____

_____   _____   _____

SCORE [   ]

B. Your mother wants you to go shopping for her. You're supposed to buy milk, eggs, and butter at the supermarket. She reminds you to be careful and not to lose the money. Write what she says. Write four sentences, using such words as **doch, bitte,** and **mal.**
4 points

_____
(1)
_____
(2)
_____
(3)
_____
(4)

SCORE [   ]

C. Read the incomplete dialog between Steffi and her mother. Complete it by filling in each blank with an appropriate word from the boxed list.
7 points

---
auf — brauchst — Brot — einkaufen — Fleisch — frisch — Geld —
Gemüse — im — Kauf — Obst — Semmeln — Sorge — Zettel

FRAU HUBER   Steffi, geh doch bitte mal für mich _____!
(1)

STEFFI   Ja, gut, Mutti. Was _____ du denn?
(2)

FRAU HUBER   Schau, hier ist ein _____. Kauf nicht alles _____
(3)   (4)

Supermarkt. _____ das _____ beim Metzger und hol
(5)   (6)

das _____ und das _____ beim Gemüsehändler! Kauf
(7)   (8)

das _____ und die _____ beim Bäcker! Dort sind sie
(9)   (10)

immer _____. Pass _____ und verlier das
(11)   (12)

_____ nicht!
(13)

STEFFI   Keine _____, Mutti! Tschüs!
(14)

SCORE [   ]

D. Frau Huber asks Steffi and Flori to go shopping. Complete the dialog by filling in each blank with the appropriate form of **sollen**.
6 points

FRAU HUBER   Ihr _____ bitte zum Supermarkt gehen.
(1)

FLORI   _____ ich mit?
(2)

STEFFI   Was _____ wir alles holen?
(3)

FRAU HUBER   Ich schreibe alles auf einen Zettel. Moment mal! Du _____ bitte die
(4)

Kirschen beim Gemüsehändler holen. Die Kirschen _____ jetzt schön
(5)

sein. Und die Gemüsefrau _____ euch auch ein Kilo Tomaten geben.
(6)

SCORE [   ]

QUIZ 20 Unit 7 • Section C

Maximum Score: 26 points

A. Steffi and Flori are sightseeing in Munich. As you listen to the following exchanges, determine whether the second speaker's response is appropriate or not. Place a check mark in the appropriate row.
5 points

	1	2	3	4	5
appropriate					
not appropriate					

SCORE _____

B. Read the paragraph and determine whether the statements that follow it are true or false. Place a check mark in the appropriate column.
6 points

Steffi möchte Flori die Sehenswürdigkeiten Münchens zeigen. Aber zu blöd! Es regnet! Der Wetterbericht ist auch nicht gut. Es bleibt kühl, und es soll ab und zu regnen. Was sollen sie jetzt machen? Sollen sie zu Hause bleiben? Nein. Sie haben Regenmäntel und Regenschirme. Sie gehen! Sie essen etwas in der Stadt. Steffi kennt eine nette Imbiss-Stube. Sie kommen auch nicht so spät nach Hause. Um 9 Uhr sind sie wieder da.

		stimmt	stimmt nicht
1.	Steffi möchte Flori die Stadt München zeigen.		
2.	Der Wetterbericht ist gut. Es regnet nicht mehr.		
3.	Steffi und Flori bleiben zu Hause.		
4.	Sie brauchen die Regenmäntel und die Regenschirme.		
5.	Steffi und Flori gehen in eine Imbiss-Stube.		
6.	Sie kommen um 11 Uhr nach Hause.		

SCORE _____

C. Complete the following dialog by filling in each blank with the appropriate form of **essen.**
8 points

STEFFI   Ich _____ Bratwurst. Was _____ du, Flori?
                                    (1)   (2)

FLORI   Ich auch. Was _____ Sie, Frau Huber?
                                   (3)

FRAU HUBER   Wenn ihr Bratwurst _____, dann _____ ich Leberkäs.
                                        (4)   (5)

FLORI   Die Steffi _____ Bratwurst. Ich _____ Bratwurst und
                               (6)   (7)

     Leberkäs. Ich habe Hunger!

FRAU HUBER   Gut! Und dann _____ wir alle noch ein Eis!
                                     (8)

SCORE _____

D. Use command forms to make the following suggestions or requests. Address the people indicated.
7 points

1. Dein Bruder soll mal zu Hause bleiben.

   _____

2. Deine Freunde sollen doch etwas essen.

   _____

3. Deine Grosseltern sollen bald kommen.

   _____

4. Dein Lehrer soll mal München besuchen.

   _____

5. Deine Mutter soll bitte Obst kaufen.

   _____

6. Deine Freundin soll mal eine Pizza essen.

   _____

7. Deine Schwester soll nicht so viel fragen.

   _____

SCORE _____

QUIZ 21   Unit 9 • Section A

Maximum Score: 24 points

A. Karin is inviting her friends to the party. Some accept the invitation, while others decline. For each exchange you hear, decide whether Karin's response is appropriate or not. Place a check mark in the appropriate row.
5 points

	1	2	3	4	5
appropriate					
not appropriate					

SCORE _____

B. Here is a telephone conversation between Karin and her friend's mother, Frau Berger. The dialog is out of order. Put it into the correct order by numbering the lines in a logical sequence.
10 points

_____ Ach, schade!

_____ Am Samstag habe ich eine Party, und ich möchte die Christine einladen. Vielleicht wissen Sie es: Hat Christine am Samstag etwas vor?

_____ Auf Wiederhören, Frau Berger!

_____ Das weiss ich nicht. Sie soll jetzt aber bald kommen. Sie ruft dich dann an. Geht das?

_____ Gut. Vielen Dank, Frau Berger!

_____ Guten Tag, Frau Berger! Hier ist die Karin. Ist Christine da?

_____ Ja, Tag, Karin! Die Christine ist leider nicht da.

_____ Nichts zu danken.

_____ Was gibt's denn?

_____ Wiederhören, Karin!

SCORE _____

C. What do you say to the person or persons in each of the following situations?
5 points

1. Du möchtest den Lehrer etwas fragen.

   Herr Fischer, ich möchte _____

2. Du verstehst deine Schwester nicht.

   Ich _____

3. Du möchtest zwei Lehrer einladen.

   Fräulein Schmidt, Herr Knauer, ich _____

4. Du rufst deine Eltern um 8 Uhr an.

   Keine Sorge! Ich _____

5. Und deine Eltern sagen:

   Gut! Du rufst _____

SCORE [   ]

D. You are having a party and are inviting some friends. Two can make it and two can't. Write what each one says. Use different ways of accepting or declining invitations.
4 points

1. _____

2. _____

3. _____

4. _____

SCORE [   ]

QUIZ 22   Unit 9 • Section B

Maximum Score: 24 points

A. Karin's party is getting started. You will hear several of her friends asking questions. Unfortunately, she didn't quite catch the last word. Decide what the last word is in each case and write the number of the question in front of the word.
5 points

_____ essen?   _____ Kuchen?   _____ los?   _____ trinken?   _____ überhaupt?

SCORE [   ]

B. Karin is going shopping for some of the items she needs for the party. Her mother tells her what to get. What does she need the various items for? Complete each sentence by filling in the blank with an appropriate word from the boxed list.
7 points

1. Kauf Aufschnitt für die _____!

2. Hol Käse für die _____!

3. Wir brauchen Erdbeeren für die _____.

4. Ich brauche Zucker und Eier für den _____.

5. Hol auch Hackfleisch für die _____!

6. Geh zum Gemüsehändler und kaufe Kartoffeln für den

_____!

7. Und wir brauchen Tomaten und Fleisch für die

_____.

| Erdbeerbowle |
| Gulaschsuppe |
| Hamburger |
| Kartoffelsalat |
| Käsebrote |
| Kuchen |
| Wurstbrote |

SCORE [   ]

C. The guests at the party are telling Karin what they would like to drink. She repeats what each one says. Fill in the blanks with the correct pronouns.
6 points

MICHAELA   Für _____ einen Apfelsaft.
                                    (1)

KARIN   Gut! Für _____ einen Apfelsaft.
                                        (2)

HEIDI UND LISA   Für _____ eine Cola.
                                    (3)

KARIN   Gut! Für _____ eine Cola.
                                        (4)

FRAU BERGER   Für _____ ein Mineralwasser.
                                    (5)

KARIN   Gut! Für _____ ein Mineralwasser.
                                        (6)

SCORE ☐

D. Write the dialog for a conversation that takes place at Karin's party. You have just arrived and are asking what there is to eat and drink. You're hungry and can't wait for things to get started. What do you say?
6 points

DU   _____
                                    (1)

KARIN   _____
                                    (2)

DU   _____
                                    (3)

KARIN   _____
                                    (4)

DU   _____
                                    (5)

KARIN   _____
                                    (6)

SCORE ☐

QUIZ 23   Unit 9 • Section C

Maximum Score: 24 points

A. Karin is offering her friends something to eat or drink. Listen to the conversations and, after each one, write what the friend is going to eat or drink. You will hear each item twice.
6 points

1. _____   4. _____

2. _____   5. _____

3. _____   6. _____

SCORE [   ]

B. Read the following questions and statements. Decide which of the lettered answer choices is the most appropriate response in each case. Circle the letter of the answer you choose.
5 points

1. Möchtest du etwas essen?

   a. Danke, nein. Ich habe keinen Hunger.

   b. Danke, nein. Ich habe keinen Durst.

2. Hier, probier mal die Suppe!

   a. Sie sieht gut aus. Ist das eine Gulaschsuppe?

   b. Sie sieht gut aus. Ist das eine Erdbeerbowle?

3. Karin, gibt es noch Hamburger?

   a. Ich esse keine Hamburger.

   b. Natürlich! Isst du noch einen Hamburger?

4. Schau, es gibt Wurstbrote und auch Käsebrote!

   a. Gibt es auch Käsebrote?

   b. Ich esse lieber eine Bratwurst.

5. Alles sieht prima aus! Ich nehme eine Bratwurst, Kartoffelsalat und vielleicht auch einen Hamburger. So, und jetzt esse ich!

   a. Guten Appetit!

   b. Hast du keinen Hunger?

SCORE [   ]

C. You are being offered the following items. Decline them, using **kein.**
5 points

1. Möchtest du einen Hamburger?   Nein, _____ Hamburger für mich.

2. Möchtest du eine Suppe?   Nein, _____ Suppe für mich.

3. Möchtest du Kartoffelsalat?   Nein, _____ Kartoffelsalat für mich.

4. Möchtest du ein Wurstbrot?   Nein, _____ Wurstbrot für mich.

5. Möchtest du Bratwürste?   Nein, _____ Bratwürste für mich.

SCORE [   ]

D. At a party you are having, you offer your guests something to eat and drink. Offer two things to eat and two things to drink. Your guest declines the first and accepts the second in each case. Write the dialog.
8 points

Du _____
(1)

Gast _____
(2)

Du _____
(3)

Gast _____
(4)

Du _____
(5)

Gast _____
(6)

Du _____
(7)

Gast _____
(8)

SCORE [   ]

QUIZ 24   Unit 9 • Section D

Maximum Score: 25 points

A. Karin's friends are making suggestions about what to do at the party. Listen to the suggestions and the responses. In each case, decide whether the second speaker thinks the suggestion is a good idea or not. Place a check mark in the appropriate row.
5 points

	1	2	3	4	5
gute Idee					
keine gute Idee					

SCORE

B. Read the following dialog and determine whether the statements that follow are true or false. Place a check mark in the appropriate column.
7 points

KLAUS	Gehst du am Samstag zu Karins Party?
UWE	Na klar! Du nicht?
KLAUS	Ich weiss nicht.
UWE	Ach, komm! Alle kommen. Und du weisst, das Essen bei Frau Haupt ist immer prima!
KLAUS	Ja, das stimmt, aber...
UWE	Und die Michaela kommt auch.
KLAUS	Ja, die Michaela. Sie tanzt so toll.
UWE	Und du kennst doch den Bernd. Er ist immer so lustig.
KLAUS	Ja, seine blöden Witze.
UWE	Und Karins Eltern sind so nett.
KLAUS	Ja, ...
UWE	Und ihr Haus ist so gemütlich.
KLAUS	Ja, sie haben den tollen Partykeller ...
UWE	Also dann, bis Samstag!
KLAUS	Ja, bis Samstag!

	stimmt	stimmt nicht
1. Klaus kommt vielleicht nicht zu Karins Party.		
2. Uwe möchte gern kommen.		
3. Klaus findet Frau Haupts Essen nicht gut.		
4. Er tanzt gern mit Michaela.		
5. Er kennt Bernds Witze nicht.		
6. Er findet Karins Haus nicht gemütlich.		
7. Klaus und Uwe sind am Samstag bei Karin.		

SCORE

C. You are at Karin's party and would like to tell Karin and her mother how much you like everything. What do you say? What do Karin and her mother say? Use possessives.
4 points

Karins Freunde sind sehr nett.

Du _____
(1)

KARIN _____
(2)

Der Kuchen von Frau Haupt ist ausgezeichnet.

DU _____
(3)

FRAU HAUPT _____
(4)

SCORE [　　　]

D. Now you are visiting Karin's school and are talking to two of her friends. Complete the compliments and the students' responses by filling in each blank with the appropriate possessive.
6 points

1. DU _____ Schule ist schön.

   SCHÜLER Ja, _____ Schule ist sehr schön.

2. DU _____ Lehrer ist nett.

   SCHÜLER Ja, _____ Lehrer ist sehr nett.

3. DU Ich finde _____ Schülerzeitung Spitze.

   SCHÜLER Ja, wir finden _____ Schülerzeitung auch gut.

SCORE [　　　]

E. Write a short paragraph telling what you and your friends like to do when you have a party.
3 points

_____

_____

_____

_____

SCORE [　　　]

QUIZ 25 Unit 10 • Section A

Maximum Score: 26 points

A. These young people are telling you what they do in their free time and what they like to do when they go out. For each person you hear, jot down two things that person likes to do. Write a word or a few words to indicate the activity. You will hear each item twice.
8 points

1. Margit Dastl

_____

_____

2. Bruno Schmidlin

_____

_____

3. Uschi Schmidt

_____

_____

4. Jens Kröger

_____

_____

SCORE [   ]

B. Stefan and Sabine have made a date to meet in the city. Now they are deciding what to do. Sabine greets Stefan first. Put the dialog into the correct order by numbering the lines in a logical sequence.
7 points

_____ Gut, danke!

_____ Grüss dich, Stefan!

_____ Hm, das ist eine Idee. Aber schau, das Wetter ist so schön! Willst du nicht einen Stadtbummel machen?

_____ Ja, grüss dich, Sabine! Wie geht's?

_____ Du hast recht. Wir können dann auch in ein Gartencafé gehen und ein Eis essen.

_____ So, was sollen wir machen? Möchtest du ins Kino gehen?

_____ Eis essen! Tolle Idee! Machen wir das!

SCORE [   ]

C. Here's what your mother says. She's talking to you and your friend. What would she say if she were talking just to you? What would she say if she were talking *about* your friend? Change the verb forms and fill in the blanks.
8 points

Was wollt ihr jetzt tun? Fahrt ihr in die Stadt? Ihr könnt dort einen Stadtbummel machen. Oder geht ihr mal wieder ins Kino?

talking to you

1. Was _____ du jetzt tun? _____ du in die Stadt? Du

_____ dort einen Stadtbummel machen. Oder _____ du mal

wieder ins Kino?

talking about your friend

2. Was _____ er jetzt tun? _____ er in die Stadt? Er

_____ dort einen Stadtbummel machen. Oder _____ er mal

wieder ins Kino?

SCORE _____

D. You and a friend want to go out together and are deciding what to do. Make three suggestions, varying the way in which you make them.
3 points

1. _____

2. _____

3. _____

SCORE _____

QUIZ 26   Unit 10 • Section B

Maximum Score: 25 points

A. You will hear eight statements relating to movies. Look at the movie timetable below as you listen. Determine whether the statement is true or false and place a check mark in the appropriate row.
8 points

KINO KINO KINO

Mathäser—Filmpalast
16.00 und 18.45
Der Mann mit 2 Gehirnen
Eine tolle Komödie mit
Steve Martin!

Theatiner—Film
20,00   Gary Cooper
Zwölf Uhr mittags
Der „ultimate" Western!

Tivoli
17.00 u. 20.00   Sidney Pollack
Jenseits von Afrika
Ein wunderschöner
Abenteuerfilm!

Royal-Filmpalast
13 / 15 / 17 / 19 Uhr
Piranha 2
Action!

Gloria
14.00 / 16.30 / 19.00
Das Boot
Ein spannender Kriegsfilm!

	1	2	3	4	5	6	7	8
stimmt								
stimmt nicht								

SCORE

B. Read the questions and match each one with an appropriate answer. Write the letter of the answer in the space provided.
7 points

_____ 1. Was für ein Film ist *12 Uhr mittags?*   a. Die Scorpions.

_____ 2. Wo spielt der Film?   b. Ein Western.

_____ 3. Wer spielt in dem Film?   c. Gary Cooper.

_____ 4. Was für Konzerte hörst du am liebsten?   d. Im Theatiner-Filmtheater.

_____ 5. Welche Gruppe hörst du gern?   e. *Jenseits von Afrika.*

_____ 6. Welchen Film siehst du heute?   f. Rockkonzerte.

_____ 7. Wann fängt der Film an?   g. Um 19 Uhr.

SCORE _____

C. Complete the following sentences by filling in each blank with the correct form of **welch-**.
5 points

1. _____ Film siehst du heute?

2. _____ Filme findest du nicht gut?

3. _____ Film spielt heute im Filmpalast?

4. _____ Konzert möchtest du hören?

5. _____ Komödie ist mit Steve Martin?

SCORE _____

D. Complete the following questions by filling in each blank with the correct form of **was für ein.**
5 points

1. _____ Filme hast du am liebsten?

2. _____ Film spielt heute?

3. _____ Film möchtest du sehen?

4. _____ Gruppe ist die Gruppe Queen?

5. _____ Konzert möchtest du hören?

SCORE _____

QUIZ 27   Unit 10 • Section C

Maximum Score: 22 points

A. These young people are talking about what they like or don't like or like best of all.
Listen to what they say and, for each statement you hear, decide which is the case.
Place a check mark in the appropriate row.
7 points

	1	2	3	4	5	6	7
gern							
am liebsten							
nicht gern							

SCORE

B. Stefan is writing a composition about his likes and dislikes. Read it and determine whether
the statements that follow are true or not. Place a check mark in the appropriate column.
8 points

Was ich gern und nicht gern habe

Ich habe Musik sehr gern. Ich mag alle Rockgruppen. Am liebsten höre ich die Gruppe Queen.
Mein Lieblingssänger ist Falco, meine Lieblingssängerin ist die Nina Hagen. Ich finde sie Spitze. Ihre
Songs sind phantasievoll und nie schmalzig. Reggae und Country-Western mag ich nicht so gern, aber
Jazz finde ich Klasse!

Ich gehe auch gern ins Kino. Kriegsfilme und Science-fiction-Filme finde ich spannend und
interessant. Western finde ich auch gut. Natürlich mag ich auch Abenteuerfilme und Komödien —
besonders Komödien mit Steve Martin. Er ist mein Lieblingsschauspieler. Was habe ich nicht gern?
Liebesfilme. Ich finde sie langweilig und oft zu traurig. Und ich hasse Filme, die zu schmalzig sind!

	stimmt	stimmt nicht
1. Stefan hört Rockgruppen gern.		
2. Seine Lieblingsgruppe ist die Gruppe Queen.		
3. Er findet Falco nicht gut.		
4. Nina Hagen findet er schmalzig.		
5. Jazzmusik mag er sehr gern.		
6. Kriegsfilme findet Stefan gut.		
7. Western mag er nicht.		
8. Er hasst Liebesfilme, wenn sie zu schmalzig sind.		

SCORE

C. What do you like and dislike? Answer the following questions. Write complete sentences.

7 points

1. Was für Filme siehst du gern?

   _____

2. Wie findest du Kriegsfilme?

   _____

3. Siehst du Science-fiction-Filme gern? Warum? Warum nicht?

   _____

4. Wie heisst dein Lieblingsstar?

   _____

5. Was hörst du lieber, Rock oder Country-Western?

   _____

6. Welchen Sänger hast du am liebsten?

   _____

7. Welche Gruppen hörst du besonders gern?

   _____

SCORE [   ]

QUIZ 28   Unit 10 • Section D

Maximum Score: 24 points

A. Are these young people talking about what they plan to do or about what they have already done? Listen to what they say and decide which it is in each case. Place a check mark in the appropriate row.
10 points

	1	2	3	4	5	6	7	8	9	10
going to do										
have already done										

SCORE [ ]

B. Sabine is talking to her friend Karin. Put the dialog into the correct order by numbering the lines in a logical sequence. The first line of the dialog is numbered for you.
7 points

_____ Den Film mit Steve Martin.

___1___ Du, Karin, möchtest du ins Kino gehen?

_____ Habt ihr wieder Karten gespielt?

_____ Ich habe ihn schon gesehen.

_____ Ich habe sie gestern besucht.

_____ Na, klar! Wie immer!

_____ Was zeigen sie?

_____ Wir können die Moni besuchen.

SCORE [ ]

C. Someone is asking your friends and you if you would like to do certain things, but you have already done everything. Write what you would say, using the conversational past and appropriate pronouns (**ich, wir,** and so on).
7 points

1. Möchtest du das Buch lesen?

   _____

2. Möchte dein Freund in die Stadt fahren?

   _____

3. Möchte deine Schwester ins Kino gehen?

   _____

4. Möchtet ihr den Film sehen?

   _____

5. Möchtest du etwas essen?

   _____

6. Möchtest du etwas trinken?

   _____

7. Möchten deine Eltern Karten spielen?

   _____

SCORE [   ]

QUIZ 29 Unit 11 • Section A

Maximum Score: 21 points

A. Andrea and Monika are talking about presents. For each sentence you hear, write the person mentioned in it under the picture of the suggested gift.
10 points

_____   _____   _____

_____   _____   _____

_____   _____   _____

_____

SCORE ⬚

B. Read the statements and pick an appropriate gift for each person from the list given. Write the letter of the gift in the space provided.
5 points

_____ 1. Mein Vater liest gern, aber er hat so viele Bücher und er hat auch nie Zeit.

_____ 2. Unsere Eltern haben meinem Bruder einen Plattenspieler geschenkt.

_____ 3. Mein Onkel macht bald eine Reise nach Amerika.

_____ 4. Meine Grossmutter bekommt immer sehr viele Blumen.

_____ 5. Meine Schwester hört gern Musik in ihrem Zimmer, wenn sie Hausaufgaben macht.

a. ein Armband
b. Blumen
c. eine Brieftasche
d. ein Buch auf Kassette
e. einen Kalender
f. eine schöne Platte
g. Pralinen
h. ein Radio
i. eine hübsche Vase

SCORE _____

C. You ask the following people what presents they are buying for their parents and they respond. Write the mini-dialogs, using appropriate possessives in the question and in the response.
6 points

1. ein Klassenkamerad

A: _____

B: _____

2. zwei Freunde

A: _____

B: _____

3. dein Lehrer

A: _____

B: _____

SCORE _____

QUIZ 30　　Unit 11 • Section B

Maximum Score: 33 points

A. You are in the department store where Andrea and Monika are shopping. You overhear Monika and the sales clerk talking. Listen to what they say and, for each speech, determine who is talking, the sales clerk or Monika. Place a check mark in the appropriate row.
10 points

	1	2	3	4	5	6	7	8	9	10
Verkäuferin										
Monika										

SCORE

B. Look at the clothing ad and answer the questions that follow with one or two words.
7 points

Jetzt für den Sommer kaufen!
DM 10,00
in Grün, Rot, Blau und Weiss
DM 18,00
ANGEBOT:
zwei　für DM 20,00!
SCHICK! Und in allen Farben!
DM 15,00
DM 6,00
DM 6,00　Für Ihre Mutter!
Für Ihren Vater!
Jeder　nur　DM 60,00

1. Was sollst du jetzt schon für den Sommer kaufen? _____

2. Gibt es die Pullis in Gelb? _____

3. Was ist im Angebot? _____

4. Für wen sollst du ein Halstuch kaufen? _____

5. Was kannst du deinem Vater schenken? _____

6. Was kosten die Mäntel? _____

7. Was kostet ein Hemd? _____

SCORE

C. Monika is asking the prices of the items listed. The sales clerk has the price list you see. Complete Monika's questions, using the appropriate form of **dies-**. Write what the sales clerk answers, using the appropriate form of **jed-** or **all-**.
8 points

Heute im Angebot	
Hemden	DM 12,00
Schuhe	DM 20,00
Mäntel	DM 60,00
Krawatten	DM 6,00

MONIKA: VERKÄUFERIN:

1. Was kostet _____? _____

2. Was kosten _____? _____

3. Was kostet _____? _____

4. Was kostet _____? _____

SCORE [   ]

D. Now the sales clerk is asking Monika if she is going to buy each of the items she inquired about. Write what the sales clerk asks, using the appropriate form of **dies-**. Write what Monika answers, using the appropriate demonstrative pronoun.
8 points

VERKÄUFERIN: MONIKA:

1. Nehmen Sie _____? Nein, _____ nehme ich nicht.

2. Nehmen Sie _____? Nein, _____ nehme ich nicht.

3. Nehmen Sie _____? Ja, _____ nehme ich.

4. Nehmen Sie _____? Ja, _____ nehme ich auch.

SCORE [   ]

QUIZ 31   Unit 11 • Section C

Maximum Score: 28 points

A. These young people are mentioning the dates of different occasions. For each one, check if the date written corresponds to what you hear. Write **ja** next to the date if it corresponds and **nein** if it doesn't.
6 points

_____ 1. am 2. März

_____ 2. am 12. Juli

_____ 3. am 10. Juni

_____ 4. am 1. Mai

_____ 5. am 29. September

_____ 6. am 30. Januar

SCORE [   ]

B. Read the following dialog and complete it by filling in the blanks with forms of appropriate verbs from the boxed list. All verbs should be in the conversational past tense. Use each verb only once.
12 points

essen — geben — haben — kaufen — schenken — sein

A: Meine Mutter hat morgen Geburtstag.

B: Was gibst du ihr? Meine Mutter _____ im März Geburtstag _____.
   (1)   (2)

Ich _____ ihr Blumen _____.
   (3)   (4)

A: Hm, was soll ich ihr bloss schenken?

B: Schenk ihr doch Pralinen!

A: Ich _____ ihr zu Weihnachten Pralinen _____.
   (5)   (6)

B: Kauf ihr doch eine Platte!

A: Meine Schwester _____ ihr eine Platte zum Muttertag _____.
   (7)   (8)

B: Lad sie zum Essen ein! In der Stadt ist ein neues Restaurant. _____ ihr schon in
   (9)

diesem Restaurant _____?
   (10)

A: Nein, das ist eine Idee. Wir _____ nie in diesem Restaurant _____.
   (11)   (12)

SCORE [   ]

C. Here are pictures from a department store ad. Write an appropriate caption for each picture. Suggest an occasion to give the item and a person to give it to.
5 points

Geschenkideen

1.
2.
3.
4.
5.

1. _____

2. _____

3. _____

4. _____

5. _____

SCORE ☐

D. Write how you would express good wishes on the following occasions.
5 points

1. Hochzeitstag _____

2. Geburtstag _____

3. Weihnachten _____

4. Muttertag _____

5. Vatertag _____

SCORE ☐

NAME _____ KLASSE _____ DATUM _____

UNIT 1 TEST

PART ONE   Listening

Maximum Score: 30 points

A. You will hear several sequences of numbers. For each sequence, write the number that
comes next. For example, you hear, **vier, fünf, sechs.** You write the number seven.
Write the numeral, not the word.
6 points

EX. __7__   1. __4__   2. __14__   3. __20__   4. __9__   5. __7__   6. __12__

SCORE [ ]

B. You will hear ~~five~~ *six* phrases. Each one is either a way of saying hello or a way of
saying goodbye. For each phrase you hear, place a check mark in the appropriate row.
For example, you hear the phrase **Guten Morgen!** You place your check mark in the
row labeled *saying hello,* because **Guten Morgen!** is a greeting.
6 points

	Ex.	1	2	3	4	5	6
saying hello	✔	✔		✓	✓		✓
saying goodbye			✓	✓		✓	

Guten Tag
Tschüs
Grüss Dich
Biss dann
Auf Wiedersehen
Morgen

SCORE [ ]

C. Listen to the following statements and questions. Determine whether the person being
addressed or talked about is male or female, and place a check mark in the
appropriate row. For example, you hear the greeting **Guten Tag, Frau Meier!** You
mark the box labeled *female,* because the person addressed, Frau Meier, is a woman.

	Ex.	1	2	3	4	5	6	7	8	9	10
male			✓	✓			✓		✓	✓	
female	✔	✓			✓	✓		✓			✓

¹ Frau Meier
² Michael
³ Junge
⁴ Sie–Sabine
⁵ Mädchen
⁶ Herr
⁷ die Lehrer
⁸ der Deutschlehr...
⁹ Er ist fünfzehn

¹⁰ Sie ist aus Deutschland

SCORE [ ]

D. You will hear eight questions, each followed by a response. Determine whether the response is appropriate or not and place a check mark in the appropriate row. For example, you hear the question **Wie alt bist du?** and the response **Ich bin der Stefan.** You place a check mark in the row labeled *not appropriate,* because the answer is not an appropriate response to the question.
8 points

1. alt - aus
2. er - sie
3. istalt - istalt
4. ist alt - istalt
5. Wie alt sind -
    sie sind
6. wie heisse du? - ich heisse
7. woher ist - er ist aus

8. Woher ist Wiebbe?
   Sie ist aus
   Deutschland

	Ex.	1	2	3	4	5	6	7	8
appropriate				✓	✓	✓	✓	✓	✓
not appropriate	✓	✓	✓						

SCORE [   ]

PART TWO   Reading

Maximum Score: 20 points

A. Read the statements and questions on the left and select a logical response for each one from the list on the right. Write the letter of the correct response in the space provided.
10 points

_____ 1. Sind Sie der Deutschlehrer? *g*

_____ 2. Ich bin vierzehn Jahre alt. *d*

_____ 3. Woher ist Jens? *b*

_____ 4. Wer ist das? *a*

_____ 5. Tag, Ralf! *c*

_____ 6. Auf Wiedersehen, Frl. Seifert! *j*

_____ 7. Wie alt bist du? *h*

_____ 8. Bist du aus der Schweiz? *f*

_____ 9. Und sind Fritz and Maria auch aus der DDR? *e*

_____ 10. Das Mädchen heisst Frederike Friedemann. *i*

a. Das ist der Stefan.
b. Er ist aus Niebüll.
c. Grüss dich, Andreas!
d. Ich auch.
e. Ja, sie sind aus Dresden.
f. Nein, aus der DDR.
g. Nein, ich bin der Mathematiklehrer.
h. Sechzehn. Und du?
i. Wie bitte? Wie heisst sie?
j. Wiedersehen!

SCORE [   ]

B. Two young people meet at a youth hostel in Austria. Put their conversation into the
correct order: number the sentences in a logical sequence.
10 points

1 _____ Auch fünfzehn. Kommst du aus Deutschland? *5*

2 _____ Aus Deutschland. Ist der Junge da auch aus der Schweiz? *7*

3 _____ Fünfzehn. Und du? *4*

4 _____ Grüss dich! Ich heisse Frank Hofer. Wie heisst du? *1*

5 _____ Ich heisse Marianne Feldmann. *2*

6 _____ Ja. Er heisst Roger Mittelbacher. *8*

7 _____ Nein, aus der Schweiz. Woher kommst du? *6*

8 _____ Roger Mittelbacher. *10*

9 _____ Wie alt bist du? *3*

10 _____ Wie bitte? Wie heisst er? *9*

SCORE [   ]

PART THREE   Writing

Maximum Score: 50 points

A. Write out the numbers in German.
10 points

BEISPIEL   15 _____**fünfzehn**_____

1. 3 *drei*

2. 8 *acht*

3. 12 *zwölf*

4. 20 *zwanzig*

5. 19 *neunzehn*

6. 11 *elf*

7. 4 *vier*

8. 16 *sechzehn*

9. 1 *eins*

10. 5 *fünf*

SCORE [   ]

B. Write four ways of saying hello and four ways of saying goodbye in German.
8 points

1. _Guten Morgen_
2. _Morgen_
3. _Gross Dich_
4. _Hallo_

1. _Auf Wiedersehen_
2. _Wiedersehen_
3. _Tschau_
4. _Tschüss_
Biss Dann

SCORE [ ]

C. Write one way you could say hello and one way you could say goodbye to each of the following people.
6 points

1. your classmate
   a. _Hallo Natalie_
   b. _Biss Dann_

2. your teacher
   a. _Guten Tag Frau_
   b. _Auf Wiedersehen_

3. the principal of your school
   a. _Guten Morgen_
   b. _Auf Wiedersehen_

SCORE [ ]

D. Complete the following paragraph by filling in each blank with the correct form of
sein.
5 points

Ich heisse Silke, und ich _____ fünfzehn. Das
                                    (1)

_____ der Michael, er _____ vierzehn. Sabine und
        (2)   (3)

Udo _____ sechzehn. Und wie alt _____ du?
            (4)   (5)

SCORE ☐

E. Write how you would ask the following questions.
6 points

1. Ask your teacher where he or she is from.

_____

2. Ask your new neighbor's son, who is your age, what his name is.

_____

3. Ask the bus driver if his name is Schulz.

_____

SCORE ☐

F. Write an appropriate question for each answer.
6 points

1. _____ Ich heisse Claudia.

2. _____ Das ist Frau Meier.

3. _____ Der Lehrer heisst Sperling.

4. _____ Ja, das ist die Deutschlehrerin.

5. _____ Ja, fünfzehn.

6. _____ Nein, aus Deutschland.

SCORE ☐

G. Write a paragraph about Jens Kröger and one about Margit Dastl. Using the information given, write three complete sentences for each one. Then write three sentences about yourself, saying what your name is, how old you are, and where you are from.
9 points

1. Jens Kröger, 15
   Niebüll, Deutschland

2. Margit Dastl, 14
   Wien, Österreich

1. Das ist _____

_____

_____

2. Das _____

_____

_____

3. Ich _____

_____

_____

SCORE [   ]

PART FOUR Culture (optional)

Maximum Score: 5 extra points

Next to each town or city, write the country in which it is located. Write in German.
5 points

1. Niebüll _____

2. Zimmerwald _____

3. Wien _____

4. Dresden _____

5. München _____

SCORE [   ]

UNIT 2 TEST

PART ONE Listening

Maximum Score: 33 points

A. You are in a stationery store and overhear the following comments and questions. Do they refer to one item or person or to more than one? Place a check mark in the appropriate row.
10 points

	1	2	3	4	5	6	7	8	9	10
one										
more than one										

SCORE [ ]

B. You will hear someone announce the times that various activities start. Write the number of the announcement under the clockface that shows the time mentioned.
10 points

_____ _____ _____ _____ _____

_____ _____ _____ _____ _____

SCORE [ ]

C. Here is Paul's report card. Listen to what grade he has in each subject and write it in the appropriate space.

9 points

Name der Schule und Schulort: _____

Schulart bzw. Schultyp: _____ *Hauptschule* _____

ZEUGNIS

_____ geb. am *7. 1. 1975*

für _____ *1.* Halbjahr

Schuljahr 19 *87, 88*   Klasse ____ *6B* ____

L E I S T U N G E N

Pflichtunterricht

Religion · · · · · · · · · _____

Deutsch · · · · · · · · · · _____

Latein · · · · · · · · · · · _____

Geschichte · · · · · · · _____

Geographie · · · · · · · _____

Sozialkunde · · · · · · · _____

Englisch · · · · · · · · · · _____

(Fachleistungskurs) · _____

Mathematik · · · · · · · _____

(Fachleistungskurs) · · _____

Physik · · · · · · · · · · · _____

Chemie · · · · · · · · · · _____

Biologie · · · · · · · · · · _____

Musik · · · · · · · · · · · _____

Kunst · · · · · · · · · · · _____

Werken · · · · · · · · · · _____

Arbeitslehre: · · · · · · · _____

Technisches Werken · · · _____

Textilarbeit · · · · · · · · _____

Hauswirtschaft · · · · · · _____

Sport · · · · · · · · · · · _____

Schrift und Form · · · · · _____

Anm.: Im Fachleistungskurs A werden erhöhte Anforderungen gestellt.

SCORE [ ]

D. Listen to the following conversations. Write the number of the conversation under the picture that shows the situation.
4 points

_____

_____

_____

_____

SCORE [   ]

Maximum Score: 15 points

A. Nicola Junghans lives in Berlin. Read the paragraph she has written about herself. Then read the questions below and, for each one, circle the letter of the correct answer.
5 points

Ich heisse Nicola Junghans. Ich gehe auf die Oberschule in Berlin. Die Schule heisst Kennedy-Schule. Die Schule ist nicht leicht. In Mathe habe ich eine Zwei und auch in Physik. Englisch und Deutsch sind schwer! Ich habe Frau Westermann in Englisch und Deutsch. Frau Westermann ist gut, aber ich bin nicht so gut! Ich habe nur eine Vier in Englisch und Deutsch. Das ist schade!

1. Wo ist die Kennedy-Schule?

   a. in Wien

   b. in Neuss

   c. in Berlin

2. Was hat Nicola in Physik und in Mathematik?

   a. eine Zwei

   b. eine Eins

   c. eine Vier

3. Hat Nicola eine Zwei in Deutsch?

   a. nein

   b. ja

4. Wie heisst Nicolas Englischlehrerin?

   a. Westermann

   b. Junghans

   c. Kennedy

5. Ist Nicolas Schule leicht oder schwer?

   a. leicht

   b. schwer

SCORE ☐

B. Here is Nicola's class schedule. Below are questions and answers based on the schedule. Referring to Nicola's schedule, select the correct answer to each question and write the number of the question in front of the answer.
10 points

STUNDENPLAN

Name **Nicola Junghans** Klasse **9c** Schule **Kennedy-Schule**

Zeit	Montag	Dienstag	Mittwoch	Donnerstag	Freitag	Sonnabend
7.45–8.25	Religion	Deutsch	Mathe	Englisch	Biologie	Deutsch
8.30–9.15	Deutsch	Deutsch	Musik	Geographie	Englisch	Geschichte
9.15–9.45	—	—	Pause	—	—	—
9.45–10.30	Englisch	Mathe	Englisch	Deutsch	Latein	Mathe
10.35–11.20	Latein	Geschichte	Französisch	Französisch	Geographie	—
11.20–11.35	—	—	Pause	—	—	—
11.35–12.20	Sport	Französisch	Latein	—	Kunst	—
12.25–1.10	Sport	—	Physik	—	Kunst	—

_____ 1. Wie heisst Nicolas Schule?

_____ 2. In welche Klasse geht sie?

_____ 3. Wann beginnt die Schule?

_____ 4. Wann ist sie aus?

_____ 5. Was hat Nicola am Donnerstag?

_____ 6. Wann hat sie Kunst?

_____ 7. Wann hat sie Sport?

_____ 8. Wann hat sie Pause?

_____ 9. Hat Nicola Sonnabend frei?

_____ 10. Lernt Nicola Spanisch?

a. Am Montag.
b. Nein, sie lernt Englisch, Französisch und Latein.
c. Um Viertel vor acht.
d. Nein, sie hat bis halb elf Schule.
e. In die 9c.
f. Von Viertel nach neun bis Viertel vor zehn und von zwanzig nach elf bis elf Uhr fünfunddreissig.
g. Um zehn nach eins.
h. Die Kennedy-Schule.
i. Am Freitag.
j. Englisch, Geographie, Deutsch und Französisch.

SCORE _____

A. You are buying school supplies and would like to know what various items cost. For the item or items pictured, write how you would ask the price. Then write what the salesperson would answer, using the appropriate pronoun to refer to the item or items.

18 points

DM 1,20

1.
a. _____

b. _____

2.
a. _____

DM 18,—
b. _____

DM 20,—

3.
a. _____

b. _____

4.
a. _____

DM 4,—
b. _____

DM 13,—
5.
a. _____

b. _____

6.
a. _____

b. _____

DM 5,—

7.
a. _____

b. _____

DM 6,—

8.
a. _____

b. _____

DM 1,10

9.
a. _____

b. _____

DM 1,—

SCORE [   ]

B. These young people are talking about the subjects they have next. Complete the dialog by filling in each blank with the correct form of **haben.**

6 points

A: Peter _____ jetzt Mathe. Und was _____ du?
         (1)   (2)

B: Ich _____ jetzt Latein.
         (3)

A: Und ihr? Was _____ ihr?
                       (4)

C: Wir _____ jetzt Geschichte.
         (5)

Andrea und Sabine _____ auch Geschichte.
                             (6)

SCORE [ ]

C. Using the pictures as cues, write how the following people get to school. Write complete sentences.

6 points

1. Wiebke _____
   _____

2. Jens _____
   _____

3. Margit _____
   _____

4. Lars und Monika _____
   _____

5. Frl. Seifert _____
   _____

6. Ich _____
   _____

SCORE [ ]

D. You and your friends are discussing school. Write an appropriate reaction to each of the following comments.
6 points

1. Ich habe eine Vier in Mathe.

_____

2. Barbara hat eine Eins in Englisch.

_____

3. Eine Fünf in Bio! Biologie ist schwer!

_____

4. Ich habe heute eine Klassenarbeit.

_____

5. Ich habe eine Sechs in Physik.

_____

6. Er hat eine Zwei in Chemie.

_____

SCORE ☐

E. You are in a stationery store buying school supplies. Write a dialog. Get the salesperson's attention and ask the price of the notebooks. Don't forget to be polite.
6 points

Du _____
                          (1)

VERKÄUFER/IN _____
                          (2)

Du _____
                          (3)

VERKÄUFER/IN _____
                          (4)

SCORE ☐

F. Write a paragraph about yourself. Include the following information:

- where you go to school
- how you get there
- some subjects you have
- a subject that is hard
- one that is easy
- the subjects you are good in
- the subjects you are not so good in
- when you have German
- the name of your German teacher
- your grade in German (as it would be expressed in a German school)

10 points

_____

_____

_____

_____

_____

_____

_____

_____

_____

_____

SCORE ☐

Read the following incomplete statements. Decide which of the lettered answer choices correctly completes each statement. Circle the letter.
5 points

1. Die Schule beginnt um _____.

   a. 8 Uhr

   b. 9 Uhr

   c. 10 Uhr

2. Die Schule ist um _____ aus.

   a. 11 Uhr

   b. 1 Uhr

   c. 3 Uhr

3. Die Noten sind _____.

   a. A, B, C, D, F

   b. 1, 2, 3, 4, 5, 6

4. Die Note Eins ist _____.

   a. sehr gut

   b. gut

   c. nicht gut

5. 9a ist Jens' _____.

   a. Note

   b. Klasse

   c. Schule

SCORE _____

UNIT 3 TEST

PART ONE Listening

Maximum Score: 35 points

A. What are these young people doing? For each statement you hear, write the number of the sentence below the corresponding picture.
10 points

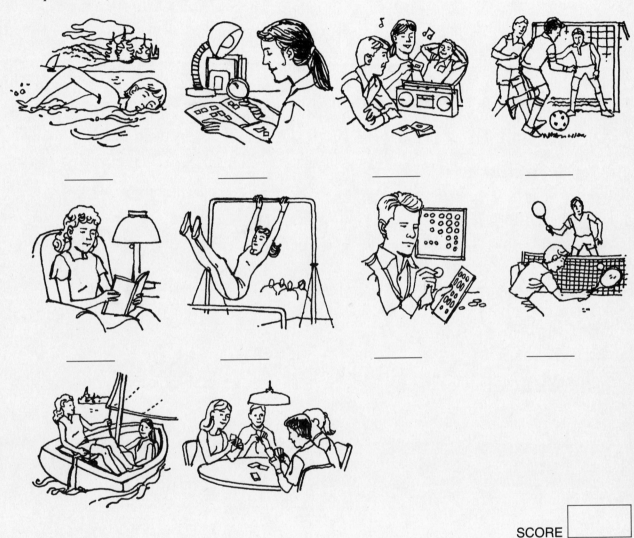

SCORE [ ]

B. You will hear ten statements. For each one, decide whether the speaker likes or dislikes the activity being discussed. Place a check mark in the appropriate row.
10 points

	1	2	3	4	5	6	7	8	9	10
likes										
dislikes										

SCORE [ ]

C. Listen to the following short conversations. For each one, decide whether the second speaker agrees or disagrees with what the first speaker says. Place a check mark in the appropriate row.
5 points

	1	2	3	4	5
agrees					
disagrees					

SCORE

D. Who are you talking to? Listen to the following questions and determine whether they are addressed to (a), (b), or (c). Place a check mark in the column under the appropriate picture.
10 points

(a)	(b)	(c)

	(a)	(b)	(c)
1.			
2.			
3.			
4.			
5.			
6.			
7.			
8.			
9.			
10.			

SCORE

PART TWO   Reading

Maximum Score: 20 points

A. Read the following short conversations and determine whether the second speaker's response is appropriate or not. Write **ja** or **nein** in the space provided.
5 points

_____ 1. A: Schach ist zu schwer. Ich spiele nicht gern. Ich verliere immer.

B: Ich finde Schach interessant. Ich bin gut, und ich gewinne oft.

_____ 2. A: Tennis ist Spitze! Ich spiele fünfmal in der Woche!

B: Wirklich? Du spielst Tennis?

_____ 3. A: Im Sommer schwimme ich meistens einmal am Tag.

B: Ich auch. Ich laufe einmal am Tag Schi.

_____ 4. A: Am liebsten spiele ich Fussball.

B: Ich spiele lieber Basketball.

_____ 5. A: Spielst du ein Instrument?

B: Ja, Gitarre.

SCORE [   ]

B. What are these young people saying? Complete the comments by filling in each blank with an appropriate word from the boxed list.
5 points

am	Comics	Freunde	gern	gewinnt
hören	Karten	liebsten	mogelst	sauer

1. Ich bin _____. Ich spiele _____ Karten, aber ich verliere immer!

2. Du gewinnst immer, aber du bist nicht gut — du _____!

3. Was liest du am _____? _____? Ich lese lieber Romane.

4. Wiebke besucht _____ Wochenende _____. Sie

_____ Musikkassetten und spielen _____. Wiebke spielt gern —

sie _____ auch immer!

SCORE [   ]

HBJ material copyrighted under notice appearing earlier in this work.

UNIT 3 TEST   **81**

Name: _Markus Walden_

	Was?	Wann?					Wie oft?								
		im Frühjahr	im Sommer	im Herbst	im Winter	am Wochenende	nie	selten	manchmal	oft	immer	am Tag	in der Woche	im Monat	im Jahr
am liebsten	Fussball		✓	✓		✓				✓			2x		
	Basketball	✓			✓						✓		1x		
lieber	Windsurfen		✓			✓			✓					4x	
	Segeln		✓	✓					✓					1x	
gern	Volleyball	✓								✓			1x		
	Gymnastik				✓					✓			3x		
nicht gern	Handball				✓			✓						1x	
	Golf		✓					✓							1x

	stimmt	stimmt nicht
1. Markus spielt Handball am liebsten.		
2. Er spielt am Wochenende oft Fussball.		
3. Er segelt einmal im Monat.		
4. Im Frühjahr macht er Gymnastik.		
5. Golf spielt er zweimal in der Woche.		
6. Er hat Basketball nicht gern. Er spielt nie.		
7. Im Sommer segelt er manchmal.		
8. Windsurfen macht er viermal am Tag.		
9. Er macht selten Gymnastik.		
10. Volleyball macht er gern. Er spielt oft im Frühjahr.		

SCORE

PART THREE   Writing

Maximum Score: 45 points

A. Write how you would ask the people below if they participate in sports, if they play guitar, and if they collect stamps. Be sure to use the appropriate form of address.
9 points

1. Wiebke

     a. _____

     b. _____

     c. _____

2. Jens, Jörg, Lars

     a. _____

     b. _____

     c. _____

3. Herr Sperling

     a. _____

     b. _____

     c. _____

SCORE [ ]

B. Here is a list of sports and activities. Pick one that you like, one that you prefer, and one that you like most of all. Write complete sentences expressing this; then write which sport or activity you don't like to do.
4 points

segeln	Fussball	Karten
schwimmen	Basketball	Schach
lesen	Hockey	Briefmarken sammeln
faulenzen	Gymnastik	Musik hören

1. _____

2. _____

3. _____

4. _____

SCORE [ ]

C. Jens Kröger loves sports. Here is a page from his weekly calendar. Write what he does. Then, next to each sport, write how many times a week and on what days he does it.
8 points

10 43 WO	Oktober 19—
24 MO	*Schwimmen* 298-68
SA 7 01 SU 17 10	
25 DI	*Basketball* 299-67
26 MI	*Schwimmen* 300-66
27 DO	*Tennis* 301-65
28 FR	*Schwimmen* 302-64
29 SA	*Fussball* 303-63
30 SO	*Fussball* 304-62

	Was?	Wie oft?	Wann?
1.			
2.			
3.			
4.			

SCORE

D. Complete the following dialogs by filling in each blank with the correct form of the appropriate verb.
20 points

INTERVIEWER   Du, Margit, _____ du Sport?
                                    (1)

MARGIT   Ja, ich _____ Gymnastik. Gymnastik _____ Spass!
                              (2)   (3)

INTERVIEWER   Und _____ du auch Hobbys?
                                (4)

MARGIT   Ja, ich _____ Münzen.
                          (5)

INTERVIEWER   Paul und Robert, _____ ihr auch Münzen?
                                          (6)

PAUL   Nein, wir _____ Briefmarken.
                        (7)

ROBERT   Was?! Ich nicht. Sammeln ist blöd!

INTERVIEWER   Wirklich? Wie _____ ihr Tennis?
                                      (8)

ROBERT   Tennis _____ wir toll!
                        (9)

PAUL   Ja, du _____ Tennis toll — ich nicht!
                      (10)

INTERVIEWER   Frau Meier, was _____ Sie in der Freizeit?
                                        (11)

FRAU MEIER   Ich _____ viel, am liebsten Romane.
                            (12)

INTERVIEWER   _____ Sie Hobbys? _____ Sie ein Instrument?
                        (13)   (14)

FRAU MEIER   Ja, ich _____ Gitarre, und ich _____ oft
                              (15)   (16)
Musikkassetten.

INTERVIEWER   Und wie _____ Sie Sport?
                                (17)

FRAU MEIER   Ich _____ Sport gern. Im Winter _____
                            (18)   (19)

ich Schi, und im Sommer _____ ich. Segeln ist prima!
                                      (20)

SCORE

E. Write what you would say if you agreed with the following statements. Then write what you would say if you disagreed. Vary the way you agree or disagree.
4 points

1. Biologie ist langweilig.

   agree: _____

   disagree: _____

2. Sammeln ist interessant.

   agree: _____

   disagree: _____

SCORE [   ]

PART FOUR   Culture (optional)

Maximum Score: 5 extra points

Read the following statements and circle the letter of the correct completion.
5 points

1. Thomas Mann, Heinrich Böll und Günter Grass sind deutsche _____.

   a. Zeitungen   b. Autoren   c. Romane

2. *Die Zeit, Die Nürnberger Nachrichten* und *Die Main Post* sind deutsche _____.

   a. Zeitungen   b. Zeitschriften   c. Comic-Hefte

3. *Bunte* and *Bravo* sind deutsche _____.

   a. Zeitungen   b. Zeitschriften   c. Fantasy-Bücher

4. „Max und Moritz", „Struwwelpeter" und „Asterix" sind populäre _____.

   a. Computerspiele   b. Comic-Figuren   c. Autoren von Kinderbüchern

5. Viele Jungen und Mädchen machen gern Sport. Sie haben Sport in der Schule, aber, wenn sie

   nach der Schule Sport machen wollen, gehen sie _____.

   a. in ein Gymnasium   b. in eine Berufsschule   c. in einen Sportverein

SCORE [   ]

REVIEW TEST 1 • Units 1–4

PART ONE Listening

Maximum Score: 45 points

A. You are curious about a new student you have met; you ask questions. For each question you hear, write its number next to the appropriate answer.
10 points

_____ Aus Deutschland.

_____ Eishockey!

_____ Fünfzehn.

_____ Ja, aber ich spiele lieber Fussball.

_____ Ja, Briefmarkensammeln.

_____ Ja, ich gehe auf die Waldschule.

_____ Karl-Heinz Fischer.

_____ Mit dem Rad.

_____ Spitze!

_____ Nein, ich habe eine Vier.

SCORE [   ]

B. When do you have which subject? Write the time you hear next to the appropriate subject. Write numerals, not words.
5 points

1. Deutsch _____

2. Geographie _____

3. Mathe _____

4. Geschichte _____

5. Englisch _____

SCORE [   ]

C. Do you remember the new friends you met in Unit 1? They will refresh your memory. Listen to what they say and fill in the information for each one in the spaces provided. Answer in words or phrases. You will hear each speaker twice.
20 points

1.   Name: Wiebke Nedel

   woher: _____

   wie alt: _____ Jahre

   Hobby: _____

   Schulweg: _____

2.   Name: Bruno Schmidlin

   woher: _____

   wie alt: _____ Jahre

   Hobby: _____ und _____

   Schulweg: _____

3.   Name: Margit Dastl

   woher: _____

   wie alt: _____ Jahre

   Hobby: _____ und _____

   Schulweg: _____

4.   Name: Jens Kröger

   woher: _____

   wie alt: _____ Jahre

   Hobby: _____

   Schulweg: _____

5.   Name: Kurt Langer

   woher: _____

   wie alt: _____ Jahre

   Hobby: _____

   Schulweg: _____

SCORE [ ]

D. You will hear various people answering the question **Wie spät ist es?** Write the number of the sentence under the clockface that shows the time mentioned in the sentence.
5 points

_____ _____ _____ _____ _____

SCORE [ ]

E. These young people are looking at some item as they talk to you. Listen to what they say and, for each one, write the number of the speaker under the picture of the appropriate item.
5 points

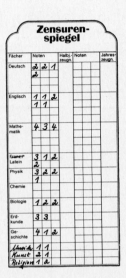

_____   _____   _____

_____

SCORE [   ]

REVIEW TEST 1   **89**

A. Read the postcards these young people have written to their friends. Then read the statements below and determine whether each one is true or false. Place a check mark in the appropriate column.
5 points

Wien

Hallo, Petra!
Ich bin in Österreich!
Wir besuchen Freunde in
Wien. Wien ist toll!

Tschüs!

Karin

Petra Baum
Bahnhofstrasse 6
79 Ulm
BRD

Schweiz • Land der Alpen

Liebe Sabine!
Herzliche Grüsse aus der
Schweiz! Das Wetter ist
phantastisch! Ich laufe jeden
Tag Schi. Wie ist das Wetter
in München? Schade, dass
Du nicht hier bist!
Wiedersehen!
Michael

Sabine Kaufmann
Widenmeyerstrasse 80
8000 München 22
BRD

	stimmt	stimmt nicht
1. Petra ist in Wien.		
2. Michael ist in der Schweiz.		
3. Sabine ist auch in der Schweiz.		
4. Karin besucht Freunde in Wien.		
5. Karin findet Wien langweilig.		

SCORE

B. Some German students are commenting on school and on the sports and activities they do. Read what they say and the statements that follow. Then, for each one, circle the letter of the answer choice that most accurately reflects either what each person said or what you can conclude from what each person said.
5 points

1. Jens: Ich finde Fussball Spitze!

   a. Er spielt Fussball gern.   b. Er spielt nie Fussball.

2. Karin: Ich habe eine Vier in Englisch.

   a. Sie ist nicht gut in Englisch.   b. Sie findet Englisch prima.

3. Thomas: Ich spiele viermal in der Woche Tennis.

   a. Er spielt selten Tennis.   b. Er spielt oft Tennis.

4. Moni: Ich habe viele Musikkassetten, und ich spiele auch Gitarre.

   a. Sie findet Musik langweilig.   b. Sie hat Musik gern.

5. Oliver: Ich finde Mathe interessant. Ich mache meine Hausaufgaben immer gern. Mein Freund und ich haben einen „Mathematik-Klub".

   a. Er ist gut in Mathe.   b. Er findet Mathe schwer.

SCORE [ ]

C. The following conversations are scrambled. Arrange each one in the correct order by numbering the sentences in a logical sequence.
13 points

1. _____ Das finde ich blöd.

   _____ Nein, Sammeln ist langweilig.

   _____ Was?! Ich sammle gern.

   _____ Sammelst du Briefmarken?

2. _____ Das ist die Schülerin aus Deutschland.

   _____ Wirklich? Wie heisst sie?

   _____ Wer ist das?

   _____ Schade!

   _____ Ich weiss nicht.

3. _____ In Mathe?

   _____ Hm, in Englisch bist du nicht gut. Viel Glück!

   _____ Ich habe eine Klassenarbeit heute.

   _____ Nein, in Englisch.

SCORE [ ]

D. Read the following paragraph, in which Annette Müller, an exchange student, tells about herself. Then answer the questions.
7 points

Ich heisse Annette Müller. Ich bin Austauschschülerin aus Deutschland. Ich besuche eine amerikanische Familie. Ich gehe auf eine Oberschule und bin in der 9. Klasse. Meine Fächer sind Deutsch, Englisch, Geschichte, Mathe, Physik, Kunst und Musik. Deutsch finde ich natürlich sehr leicht, und Englisch ist für mich auch nicht schwer. Geschichte ist schwer. Manchmal sind Mathe und Physik auch schwer, aber ich mache immer meine Hausaufgaben, und ich habe meistens gute Noten. Die Schule macht Spass! Meine Klassenkameraden und die Lehrer sind toll! Sie helfen mir immer, wenn ich Probleme habe.

1. Wer ist Annette Müller?

   _____

2. Was macht sie in Amerika?

   _____

3. Welche Fächer findet sie leicht?

   _____

4. Welche Fächer findet sie schwer?

   _____

5. Ist Annette gut in der Schule?

   _____

6. Geht Annette gern in die Schule?

   _____

7. Wie findet sie die Klassenkameraden und die Lehrer?

   _____

SCORE [   ]

PART THREE Writing

Maximum Score: 75 points

A. This poster is hanging in the window of a stationery store at the beginning of the
new school year. Fill in the plural forms of the items pictured.
9 points

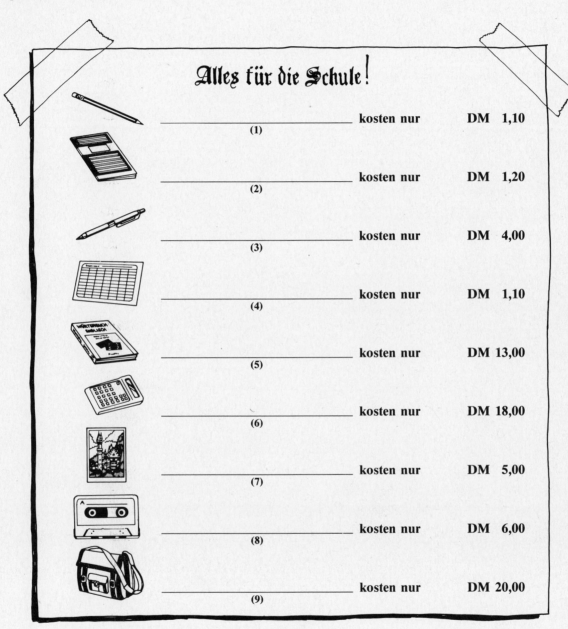

B. Two friends are looking at the poster and commenting to each other about the bargains. Complete the dialog by filling in each blank with the correct article or pronoun.
14 points

A: Schau, Willi, _____ Poster! _____ kostet nur fünf Mark!
                   (1)   **(2)**

B: Toll! Und _____ Musikkassette! _____ kostet nur sechs Mark!
             (3)   **(4)**

A: Mensch, Klasse! _____ Taschenrechner kostet acht Mark!
                  (5)

B: Quatsch! _____ kostet achtzehn Mark!
           (6)

A: Ach so! Stimmt! Aber _____ Wörterbuch kostet nur dreizehn Mark. Oder kostet _____
                        (7)   **(8)**
auch achtzehn Mark?

B: Nein, _____ kostet dreizehn Mark. Was kostet _____ Schultasche?
          (9)   **(10)**

A: _____ kostet zwanzig Mark.
    (11)

B: Schade! Zwanzig Mark habe ich heute nicht.

A: Hier, _____ Kuli. _____ kostet nur vier Mark. Hast du vier Mark?
         (12)   **(13)**

B: Ja, aber schau mal! _____ Bleistift ist auch gut und kostet nur eine Mark zehn!
                  (14)

SCORE ☐

C. You are in a store selling school supplies and would like to know the price of a dictionary. Write a dialog. Get the salesperson's attention and ask how much the dictionary costs. When the salesperson tells you it costs thirteen marks, make an appropriate comment. Be polite!
4 points

Du _____
                                           (1)

Verkäufer/in _____
                                           (2)

Du _____
                                           (3)

Verkäufer/in _____
                                           (4)

SCORE ☐

94   REVIEW TEST 1

D. The following conversations are taking place in the schoolyard. Complete each dialog by filling in each blank with the appropriate form of the verb in parentheses.
15 points

(machen)

A: Was _____ ihr heute?
           (1)

B: Wir _____ Gymnastik. Was _____ du?
         (2)   (3)

A: Ich _____ Hausaufgaben.
         (4)

(kommen)

A: Tina, wie _____ du in die Schule?
           (5)

B: Ich _____ mit dem Rad.
        (6)

A: _____ die Gabi auch mit dem Rad?
     (7)

B: Nein, sie _____ zu Fuss. Aber Karin, Uwe und Christine
         (8)

_____ alle mit dem Rad.
  (9)

(haben)

A: Ich _____ jetzt Mathe. Wir _____ eine Klassenarbeit.
        (10)   (11)

B: Wirklich? Dann _____ der Frank auch eine Klassenarbeit. Aber nach Mathe
               (12)

_____ ihr Sport.
  (13)

A: Ja, prima!

(segeln)

A: Du, Antje, _____ du?
           (14)

B: Ja, Segeln ist toll! Ich _____ gern.
               (15)

SCORE [   ]

E. What sports or activities do *you* like? For each season of the year, write a sentence telling one sport or activity you like to do in that season.
4 points

1. _____

2. _____

3. _____

4. _____

SCORE [   ]

F. Read the following paragraph about Margit Dastl. A friend of yours would like to know more about her. Write five questions your friend might ask that you could answer with information from the paragraph.
5 points

Margit Dastl ist vierzehn Jahre alt. Sie ist aus Österreich. Sie geht auf die Oberschule in Wien und kommt mit der Strassenbahn in die Schule. Margit macht gern Sport. Am liebsten macht sie Gymnastik. Sie sagt: „Gymnastik ist schwer, aber es macht Spass!"

1. _____

2. _____

3. _____

4. _____

5. _____

SCORE [   ]

G. Your school newspaper is running a series called "Getting to Know Your Teacher." You are interviewing your German teacher, Herr Gruber. Write a dialog giving your questions and Herr Gruber's answers. Be sure to cover the following points with Herr Gruber: where he is from; what his sports and hobbies are; and what sports and hobbies he likes most of all.
8 points

DU _____
(1)

HERR G. _____
(2)

DU _____
(3)

HERR G. _____
(4)

DU _____
(5)

HERR G. _____
(6)

DU _____
(7)

HERR G. _____
(8)

SCORE [   ]

H. You and your friends are talking about school, sports, and activities. Different people make comments. Some friends agree, while other disagree. For each statement, write (a) a comment agreeing with the opinion stated and (b) another one disagreeing with it. Vary your responses as much as possible.
10 points

1. Fussball ist phantastisch!

    a. _____

    b. _____

2. Mathe ist schwer.

    a. _____

    b. _____

3. Ich finde Schach langweilig.

    a. _____

    b. _____

4. Sammeln ist interessant.

    a. _____

    b. _____

5. Eine Drei ist nicht schlecht.

    a. _____

    b. _____

SCORE ☐

I. You are joining a pen-pal organization. Write a paragraph about yourself that will be used to match you with a pen pal in a German-speaking country. Include the following information:

- your name and age and where you are from
- your school and some of your subjects
- some of your sports and activities
- what you like to do most of all
6 points

_____

_____

_____

_____

_____

_____

SCORE ☐

PART FOUR Culture (optional)

Maximum Score: 10 extra points

Look at the map and locate the countries and bodies of water listed below. For each geographical feature, write the letter next to the corresponding name in the space provided.
10 points

_____ 1. Belgien

_____ 2. Bundesrepublik Deutschland

_____ 3. Dänemark

_____ 4. Deutsche Demokratische Republik

_____ 5. Frankreich

_____ 6. Italien

_____ 7. Liechtenstein

_____ 8. Luxemburg

_____ 9. Niederlande

_____ 10. Nordsee

_____ 11. Österreich

_____ 12. Ostsee

_____ 13. Polen

_____ 14. Schweiz

_____ 15. Tschechoslowakei

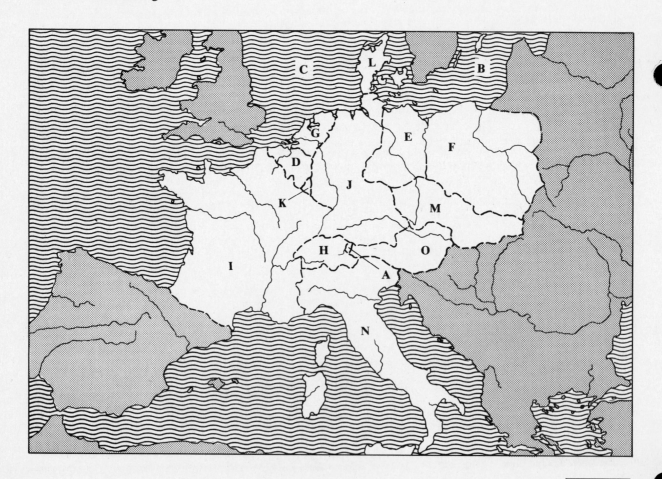

SCORE

UNIT 5 TEST

PART ONE Listening

Maximum Score: 35 points

A. You are packing for a trip to Germany. Do you have everything? Write the number of the question or comment in which you hear an item mentioned under the picture of that item.
10 points

_____

_____

_____

SCORE [   ]

B. Peter is asking for directions at the airport. Look at the diagram from Peter's point of view as you listen to the directions he is given. If the directions are correct, place a check mark in the row labeled **stimmt.** If they aren't correct, place a check mark in the row labeled **stimmt nicht.**
8 points

	1	2	3	4	5	6	7	8
stimmt								
stimmt nicht								

SCORE

C. You are listening to arrival and departure times. Write the number of the announcement under the clockface that shows the time mentioned in the announcement.
5 points

_____   _____   _____   _____   _____

SCORE

D. Frau Nedel has given Peter two telephone numbers over the phone. Did he write them down correctly? Listen to Frau Nedel and check what Peter wrote. In the space provided, write **stimmt** if it is right; correct it if it is wrong.
2 points

1. 4 52 36 _____

2. 73 87 92 _____

SCORE [   ]

E. What is Peter looking for at the airport? Listen to each group of sentences and decide which term would correctly complete it. Write the number of the sentence in front of the appropriate completion.
6 points

_____ die Auskunft   _____ die Post

_____ die Bank   _____ das Restaurant

_____ den Geschenkladen   _____ das Telefon

SCORE [   ]

F. There have been a lot of schedule and gate changes today at the airport. Check the monitor as you listen to the flight announcements. If there has been a change, circle it. If not, place a check mark in the blank next to the information posted for that announcement.
4 points

Flug	nach	Zeit	Ausgang
LH 368	Köln	12.40	B10
LH 400	Stuttgart	14.25	B8
LH 1005	Frankfurt	20.35	A58
LH 408	New York	13.15	A11

_____

_____

_____

_____

HBJ material copyrighted under notice appearing earlier in this work.

UNIT 5 TEST   **101**

PART TWO Reading

A. Peter is having a conversation with a woman he met on the plane to Frankfurt. She asks Peter about his trip. Read Peter's answers; then choose the appropriate question from the lettered choices and circle the corresponding letter.
6 points

1. Nein, ich fliege weiter nach Köln.

   a. Wie lange bleibst du?

   b. Bleibst du in Frankfurt?

   c. Bleibst du vierzehn Tage?

2. Ich besuche Freunde.

   a. Wohin fliegst du?

   b. Machst du Ferien?

   c. Was machst du in Deutschland?

3. Nein, in Neuss.

   a. Hast du auch Freunde in Neuss?

   b. Sind die Freunde in Köln?

   c. Wie heissen die Freunde?

4. Mit dem Auto.

   a. Wie kommst du nach Neuss?

   b. Fliegst du weiter?

   c. Wie weit ist es?

5. 189 Kilometer.

   a. Wie findest du Köln?

   b. Wie kommst du nach Köln?

   c. Wie weit ist es von Frankfurt nach Köln?

6. Acht Wochen.

   a. Wie alt bist du?

   b. Wie lange bleibst du in Deutschland?

   c. Wie oft fliegst du nach Köln?

SCORE ☐

B. Where were you when you overheard the following fragments of conversation? For each one, write the letter of the place in the space provided.
6 points

a. am Zoll

b. an der Passkontrolle

c. am Telefon

d. an der Auskunft

e. in der Bank

f. in der Post

_____ 1. Den Pass, bitte!

_____ 2. Hier Nedel.

_____ 3. Ich möchte 50 Dollar wechseln. Ist der Kurs heute gut?

_____ 4. Entschuldigung! Was kosten die Postkarten nach Amerika?

_____ 5. Wann geht der Flug nach Köln?

_____ 6. Ich habe nichts zu verzollen.

SCORE ☐

C. Peter is now in Neuss at the Nedels'. His father calls from New York. Wiebke answers the phone. Mr. Seber speaks briefly to Wiebke and then to Peter. The conversation is in two parts, both scrambled. Put both parts into the correct order by numbering the sentences in a logical sequence.
12 points

_____ Grüss dich, Peter! Na dann, wie findest du Deutschland und die Nedels?

_____ Guten Tag, Herr Seber! Moment mal, bitte! — Peter, der Vati aus New York!

_____ Spitze! Es ist alles toll!

_____ Hier Nedel.

_____ Vati, grüss dich!

_____ Ja, hier Helmut Seber. Tag, Wiebke! Ist der Peter da?

_____ Ja, bis Samstag. Auf Wiederhören, Vati!

_____ Gut! Du, Peter, Mutti und ich kommen am Samstag nach Köln. Wir sind um 14 Uhr da.

_____ Nach Wien! Vati, das ist toll!

_____ Zwei Wochen, dann fliegen wir alle weiter nach Wien.

_____ Na dann tschüs, Peter! Bis Samstag!

_____ Was!? Ihr kommt nach Köln? Wirklich? Wie lange bleibt ihr?

SCORE [   ]

A. Here is the list Peter wrote of things he needs for his trip. He's checking that he has everything. Fill in on the right what he says as he checks off the items on the left.
5 points

Peter: Ich habe...

das Flugticket	(1)
der Pass	(2)
die Reiseschecks	(3)
das Adressbuch	(4)
der Reiseführer	(5)
der Walkman	(6)
die Musikkassetten	(7)
das Wörterbuch	(8)
die Kamera	(9)
der Film	(10)

SCORE ☐

B. Read the following paragraph about Peter Seber and write ten questions that can be answered with the underlined information. Use as many different interrogatives as you can.
10 points

    Peter Seber kommt aus New York. Er fliegt heute nach Deutschland. Er bleibt vier Wochen in Neuss. Peter besucht dort die Familie Nedel. Peters Flug nach Köln geht um 12 Uhr 40. Herr und Frau Nedel sind im Flughafen in Köln. Sie kommen dann mit dem Auto nach Neuss. Es sind ungefähr 50 Kilometer. In Frankfurt sucht Peter die Bank. Er möchte 50 Dollar in D-Mark wechseln.

(continued on next page)

1. _____

2. _____

3. _____

4. _____

5. _____

6. _____

7. _____

8. _____

9. _____

10. _____

SCORE [   ]

C. Frau Nedel is asking Peter and Wiebke what they would like to do over the weekend. Complete the dialog by filling in each blank with the correct **möchte**-form.
7 points

FRAU NEDEL   Nun, ihr zwei, was _____ ihr am Wochenende machen?
                                    (1)

Der Philipp und die Ulrike _____ schwimmen gehen.
                                            (2)

WIEBKE   Wir _____ gern Tennis spielen.
                    (3)

FRAU NEDEL   Wirklich? Du _____ Tennis spielen, Peter?
                            (4)

PETER   Ja, ich spiele Tennis gern. _____ Sie auch spielen?
                                        (5)

FRAU NEDEL   Ja, gut. Ich _____ auch gern mal spielen.
                            (6)

WIEBKE   Toll! Ich frag' mal den Vati, dann sind wir vier. Der Vati _____ immer
                                                                            (7)

gern Tennis spielen!

SCORE [   ]

D. You are at the airport and need some help finding your way around. For each item below, write an exchange that takes place at the information desk. You ask directions to the place indicated in the pictogram. The clerk gives you directions according to the position of the arrow.

5 points

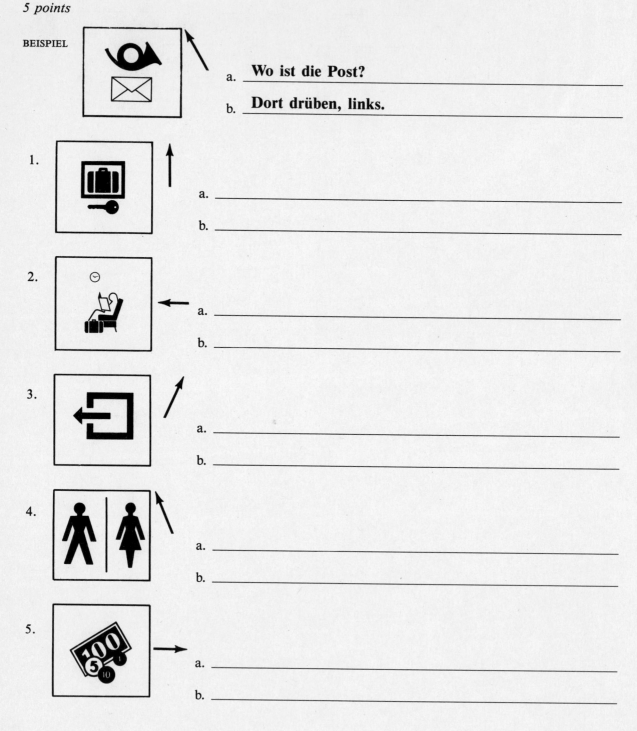

BEISPIEL

a. **Wo ist die Post?**

b. **Dort drüben, links.**

1.
a. _____
b. _____

2.
a. _____
b. _____

3.
a. _____
b. _____

4.
a. _____
b. _____

5.
a. _____
b. _____

SCORE

E. Peter calls up the Nedels to tell them he is in Frankfurt and will be arriving in Köln at 1:10 in the afternoon, flight LH 368. Frau Nedel answers the phone and tells Peter they will be there. Write the dialog.
8 points

FRAU NEDEL _____
(1)

PETER _____
(2)

FRAU NEDEL _____
(3)

PETER _____
(4)

_____
(5)

FRAU NEDEL _____
(6)

PETER _____
(7)

FRAU NEDEL _____
(8)

SCORE ☐

F. You are on your way to Germany. In the plane you sit next to a student around your own age. Write the conversation you might have with this student. Write at least six lines.
6 points

_____

_____

_____

_____

_____

_____

_____

_____

SCORE ☐

Identify the German coins and bills pictured below. Write what each one is called in German.
5 points

_____

_____

_____

_____

_____

SCORE [   ]

UNIT 6 TEST

PART ONE Listening

Maximum Score: 30 points

A. Wiebke is introducing members of her family to Peter, the guest from America, and some of Wiebke's friends are introducing themselves. Decide whether Peter's responses are appropriate or not, and place a check mark in the corresponding row.
7 points

	1	2	3	4	5	6	7
appropriate							
not appropriate							

SCORE [   ]

B. Now Wiebke is showing Peter the house and grounds. Look at the ground-floor plan and listen to what Wiebke says as she shows him around. Write the number of Wiebke's comment in the appropriate space on the diagram.
8 points

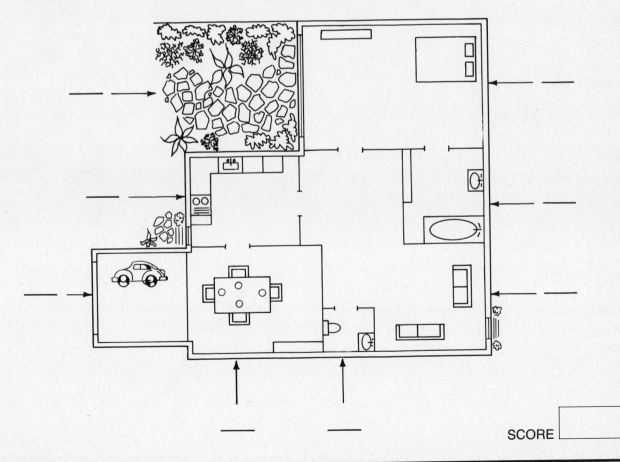

SCORE [   ]

C. Listen to the following exchanges and identify the situation. For each exchange you hear, place a check mark in the appropriate row.
10 points

	1	2	3	4	5
introducing someone					
giving a gift					
showing around the house					
describing someone					
expressing opinions about someone					

SCORE [ ]

D. Peter is checking over the presents he has for the Nedels. You will hear him say what he's giving everyone. Match the picture of the present with the person it is for. Write the letter of the present next to the name of the person.
5 points

1. _____ Hartmut

2. _____ Wiebke

3. _____ Sabine

4. _____ Ulrike

5. _____ Julian

a.

b.

c.

d.

e.

SCORE [ ]

PART TWO Reading

Maximum Score: 20 points

A. Here are some fragments of conversation overheard at the Nedels' party for Peter.
Read each statement and, for each one, circle the letter of the comment that would
logically follow.
5 points

1. Peter, das Geschenk ist toll! Vielen Dank!

   a. Bitte schön!

   b. Wie bitte?

   c. Ich weiss nicht.

2. Du, Wiebke, das Haus ist schön! So gross
   und modern!

   a. Danke!

   b. Findest du?

   c. Das stimmt nicht!

3. Ich finde die Antje sehr attraktiv.

   a. Tausend Dank!

   b. Mensch, prima!

   c. Ich auch.

4. Der Peter sieht gut aus, und er ist nett.

   a. Sieht der Peter gut aus?

   b. Schön, dass du da bist!

   c. Das stimmt! Ich finde ihn auch nett.

5. Ich bin der Jochen, ein Klassenkamerad von
   Wiebke.

   a. Bist du ein Klassenkamerad von Wiebke?

   b. Grüss dich, Jochen! Wie geht's?

   c. Kennst du die Wiebke?

SCORE [   ]

B. What or who are these young people talking about? Read each paragraph and
identify the topic. Write the corresponding letter in the space provided.
7½ points

a. meine Grosseltern   c. meine Freundin   e. mein Hund

b. der Keller   d. unser Haus

_____ 1. Sie ist sehr hübsch und sehr sympathisch. Ich finde sie auch interessant. Sie sammelt
Briefmarken, und ich sammle auch gern. Im Sommer spielen wir viel Tennis, und im
Winter laufen wir Schi.

_____ 2. Sie wohnen in der Schweiz. Ich besuche sie oft, und sie sagen dann immer: „Wie schön,
dass du da bist!"

_____ 3. Das ist der Beppo. Er ist klein und lustig. Ich finde ihn toll. Er ist immer freundlich. Im
Sommer ist er im Garten. Im Winter kommt er immer zu uns ins Wohnzimmer.

_____ 4. Es ist gross und modern. Es hat sechs Zimmer: eine Küche, ein Esszimmer, ein
Wohnzimmer und drei Schlafzimmer. Das brauchen wir: wir sind eine grosse Familie.

_____ 5. Ist er nicht toll? Klein, dunkel, gemütlich. Phantastisch für eine Party!

SCORE [   ]

C. A friend of yours is describing some people he knows. Read the descriptions and match them to the drawings. Write the name of each person under the appropriate picture.

7½ points

_____ _____ _____

_____ _____

1. Frau Hagen ist Jochens Tante. Sie ist klein und vollschlank. Sie ist brünett und hat eine Brille. Sie kommt aus Berlin.

2. Mein Freund Fritz ist Student. Er ist an der Universität München, wo er Medizin studiert. Er ist gross und blond, und er hat eine Brille. Er sieht sehr gut aus, und er ist auch sehr intelligent. Er ist aber gar nicht arrogant.

3. Mein Bruder Hans ist klein und frech! Er ist sehr schlampig und unordentlich. (Ich bin natürlich immer sehr ordentlich!) Seine Haare sehen immer wild aus. Meine Mutter sagt immer: „Ja, Hansi, wie siehst du wieder aus?! So kannst du nicht in die Schule gehen!"

4. Meine Schwester Gerda ist sehr hübsch und musikalisch. Sie spielt Gitarre und singt auch. Sie ist gross und schlank und hat langes, blondes Haar. Sie ist auch nett und hat viele Freunde.

5. Herr Krauss ist der Lehrer für Deutsch und Englisch. Er ist sehr gross, und manchmal sieht er direkt unfreundlich aus. Aber unfreundlich ist er nicht. Er ist wirklich sehr sympathisch. Seine Deutschstunden sind immer interessant, und auch Englisch macht bei ihm Spass.

SCORE [ ]

PART THREE Writing

Maximum Score: 50 points

A. You are a guest at Wiebke's gathering. Write how the following people introduce themselves to you.
4 points

1. Monika, Freundin _____

_____

2. Jochen, ein Klassenkamerad _____

_____

3. Julian, Vetter _____

_____

4. Ali, Kusine _____

_____

SCORE ☐

B. Wiebke introduces her family members to you. Write what she says and what you say.
6 points

1. Herr und Frau Graf, Grosseltern

WIEBKE _____
                                              (a)

DU _____
                                              (b)

2. Jürgen und Christa Wolf, Onkel und Tante

WIEBKE _____
                                              (a)

DU _____
                                              (b)

3. Ulrike und Philipp, Geschwister

WIEBKE _____
                                              (a)

DU _____
                                              (b)

SCORE ☐

C. Wiebke is introducing her family. Complete the following paragraph by filling in each blank with the appropriate form of **mein.**
9 points

Das ist _____ Vater, und das ist _____
　　　　　　　(1)　　　　　　　　　　　　　　　　　　　(2)

Mutter. _____ Geschwister heissen Philipp und Ulrike.
　　　　　　　(3)

_____ Tante heisst Christa Wolf, und _____
　　(4)　　　　　　　　　　　　　　　　　　　　　　　　　(5)

Onkel heisst Jürgen. Julian ist _____ Vetter, und Ali ist
　　　　　　　　　　　　　　　　(6)

_____ Kusine. _____ Grosseltern sind dort
　　(7)　　　　　　　　　　　(8)

drüben. Sie heissen Herr und Frau Graf. Und schau, hier ist _____
　　　　　　　　　　　　　　　　　　　　　　　　　　　　　　　　　(9)

Hund, der Beppo.

SCORE [　　]

D. Complete the following paragraph about Wiebke's friend Monika by filling in each blank with the appropriate form of **ein.**
4 points

Monika ist _____ Freundin von Wiebke. Sie hat
　　　　　　　(1)

_____ Bruder und _____ Schwester. Sie hat
　　(2)　　　　　　　　　　　　　　(3)

auch _____ Hund. Er heisst Waldi.
　　　　(4)

SCORE [　　]

E. Peter is checking off his list of presents. Write the correct form of **ein** in the first part of the sentence and the correct form of **der** in the second.
5 points

1. Ich habe _____ Halskette für _____ Sabine.

2. Ich habe _____ Poster für _____ Ulrike.

3. Ich habe _____ Taschenrechner für _____ Philipp.

4. Ich habe _____ Musikkassette für _____ Hartmut.

5. Ich habe _____ Buch für _____ Grosseltern.

SCORE [   ]

F. Your sister is going out. She asks you how she looks. Complete the following dialog by filling in the blanks with appropriate forms of the verb **aussehen**.
3 points

A: Wie _____ ich _____?
      (1)   (2)

B: Du _____ gut _____!
      (3)   (4)

A: Wirklich? Die Halskette _____ nicht blöd _____?
                              (5)   (6)

B: Nein, überhaupt nicht!

SCORE [   ]

HBJ material copyrighted under notice appearing earlier in this work.

UNIT 6 TEST **115**

G. A friend of Natalie's and Moni's has company from America and is giving a party. Their mother talks to the girls before they leave for the party. Complete the conversation by filling in the blanks with forms of **aussehen.**
3 points

A: Ihr _____ ja toll _____! Was macht ihr?
          (1)   (2)

B: Susanne hat eine Party. Freunde aus Amerika sind da.

A: Ach so. Sind die Freunde nett? _____ sie sympathisch _____?
                                            (3)   (4)

B: Ich weiss nicht. Wir kennen sie nicht.

C: Was meinst du, Mutti? _____ wir sympathisch _____?
                                (5)   (6)

B: Ja, sehr sympathisch!

SCORE ☐

H. Your friend comments on a variety of people and things. You respond, using a pronoun in place of the subject of conversation. Fill in each blank with the appropriate pronoun.
6 points

1. FREUND/IN Ich finde Frau Schmidt interessant.

   DU   Ich finde _____ langweilig.

2. FREUND/IN Müllers haben einen grossen Keller.

   DU   Ja, ich finde _____ prima für eine Party.

3. FREUND/IN Barbaras Grosseltern sind nett.

   DU   Ich finde _____ auch nett.

4. FREUND/IN Du hast ein sehr modernes Haus.

   DU   Ich finde _____ zu modern.

5. FREUND/IN Die Hausaufgaben sind heute sehr schwer.

   DU   Ach, ich finde _____ nicht so schwer.

6. FREUND/IN Arnolds Hund, der Fritzi, ist lustig.

   DU   Ich finde _____ auch lustig.

SCORE ☐

I. Write a description of someone you know—a member of your family, a friend, or a classmate—or make someone up. Write how that person looks, what he or she likes to do, and what you think of him or her.
4 points

_____

_____

_____

_____

SCORE [____]

J. You are showing a friend around your home, and he or she is suitably impressed. Write a dialog in which you point out four rooms and the friend makes appropriate comments on each one. Start off with yourself as the first speaker.
6 points

A: _____

B: _____

A: _____

B: _____

A: _____

B: _____

A: _____

B: _____

SCORE [____]

Match each description of a fairy tale or quote from a fairy tale with the correct title. In the space provided, write the letter of the correct title.
5 points

a. Rapunzel   c. Rotkäppchen   e. Aschenputtel

b. Rumpelstilzchen   d. Schneewittchen

_____ 1. Die böse Stiefmutter sagt: „Spieglein, Spieglein an der Wand, wer ist die schönste im ganzen Land?"

_____ 2. Das schöne Mädchen hat langes, goldenes Haar. Sie wohnt in einem Turm. Der Königssohn besucht sie.

_____ 3. Das Mädchen hat eine böse Stiefmutter und zwei böse Schwestern. Sie geht auf einen Ball und tanzt mit dem Prinzen. Sie verliert einen Schuh.

_____ 4. Der kleine Mann hilft der Müllerstochter. Er spinnt Stroh zu Gold für sie. Aber dann will er ihr erstes Kind haben. Wie heisst er?

_____ 5. Das Mädchen sagt: „Grossmutter, was hast du für grosse Augen!" Der Wolf sagt: „Damit ich dich besser sehen kann!"

SCORE [   ]

MIDTERM TEST • Units 1–6

PART ONE   Listening

Maximum Score: 50 points

A. You are spending a year as an exchange student in Germany. In the course of a day you hear different conversations. What are the different people talking about? Are they talking about school, about their leisure-time activities, about a vacation trip, about their families, or perhaps about where they live? Listen to the conversations and determine what is being talked about. Place a check mark in the appropriate row.
10 points

	1	2	3	4	5
Schule					
Freizeit					
Ferien					
Familie					
Haus					

SCORE

B. You will hear a student tell you a little about herself. Based on what she says, choose the correct answer for each question below. Take a minute now to read the questions and their suggested answers to yourself.

Now listen to what the student has to say. Then, for each question, circle the letter of the correct answer.
6 points

1. Wie alt ist Marianne?

   a. 13   b. 14   c. 15   d. 16

2. Wo wohnt sie?

   a. in Deutschland   b. in Österreich   c. in der Schweiz   d. in den USA

3. Wieviel Geschwister hat sie?

   a. zwei   b. drei   c. vier   d. fünf

SCORE

C. The student Paul Lehmann will now tell you about a trip he is taking. Based on what he says, choose the correct answer for each question below. Take a minute now to read the questions and their suggested answers to yourself.

Now listen to what Paul has to say. Then, for each question, circle the letter of the correct answer.
8 points

1. Wohin fliegt Paul?
   a. nach New York
   b. nach New Jersey
   c. nach Deutschland

2. Wen besucht er?
   a. einen Freund
   b. einen Onkel
   c. die Grosseltern

3. Wer sind Frank und Richard?
   a. Pauls Vettern
   b. Pauls Brüder
   c. Pauls Freunde

4. Wie kommt Paul von New York nach New Jersey?
   a. mit dem Flugzeug
   b. mit der Bahn
   c. mit dem Auto

SCORE

☐

D. Here is a page from Jochen Schmidt's weekly calendar. You will hear some statements about Jochen's activities. Look at the calendar as you listen to the statements. Determine whether each one is true or false, and place a check mark in the appropriate row. You will hear each item twice.
16 points

APRIL

Montag	16⁰⁰ *Tennis*	8
Dienstag	*Fussballtraining*	9
Mittwoch	16⁰⁰ *Tennis*	10
Donnerstag	14⁰⁰ *Gymnastik – toll!!* 20⁰⁰ *Party bei Antje*	11
Freitag	*Klassenarbeit – Englisch*	12
Samstag		13
Sonntag	*Tante Anni – Köln*	14

	1	2	3	4	5	6	7	8
stimmt								
stimmt nicht								

SCORE

☐

E. You will hear a number of exchanges. Match each one with the corresponding picture below. Write the number of the exchange under the picture it most logically corresponds to.
10 points

_____   _____   _____

_____   _____

SCORE [   ]

A. When you are in Germany you will come across many different things to read—signs, ads, forms, announcements, and so on. Here are some examples. Look over the various items and answer, in German, the questions that follow.
24 points

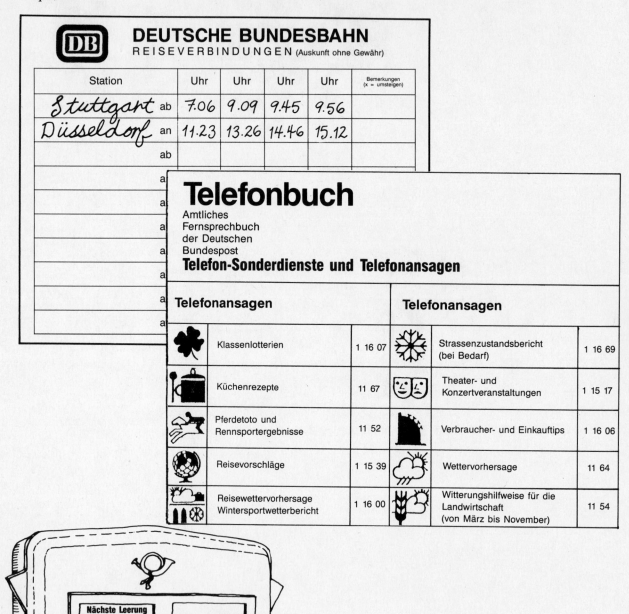

DEUTSCHE BUNDESBAHN
REISEVERBINDUNGEN (Auskunft ohne Gewähr)

Station		Uhr	Uhr	Uhr	Uhr	Bemerkungen (x = umsteigen)
Stuttgart	ab	7.06	9.09	9.45	9.56	
Düsseldorf	an	11.23	13.26	14.46	15.12	
	ab					
	an					
	ab					
	ab					
	ab					
	ab					
	ab					
	ab					

Telefonbuch
Amtliches
Fernsprechbuch
der Deutschen
Bundespost
Telefon-Sonderdienste und Telefonansagen

Telefonansagen			Telefonansagen		
🍀	Klassenlotterien	1 16 07	❄️	Strassenzustandsbericht (bei Bedarf)	1 16 69
	Küchenrezepte	11 67		Theater- und Konzertveranstaltungen	1 15 17
	Pferdetoto und Rennsportergebnisse	11 52		Verbraucher- und Einkauftips	1 16 06
	Reisevorschläge	1 15 39		Wettervorhersage	11 64
	Reisewettervorhersage Wintersportwetterbericht	1 16 00		Witterungshilfweise für die Landwirtschaft (von März bis November)	11 54

Nächste Leerung	
Montag-Freitag Samstag	7 16 An Samstagen 7 13
Sonntag	9

(continued on next page)

Für Freizeit und Hobby

Ein spezielles Taschenbuchprogramm: illustriert, modern und informativ.

ab 2.80 DM

ht 23: Tiere Afrikas
ht 68: Comics aus Frankreich
ht 143: Schach: 3 000 Fragen
ht 174: Kamera-Welt
ht 182: Sport-Quiz

Stundenplan für _Peter Woef_

Zeit	Montag	Dienstag	Mittwoch	Donnerstag	Freitag	Samstag
8 – 8.40	Mathe	Deutsch	Geo	Mathe	Latein	
8.45–9.30	Latein	Englisch	Latein	Religion	Englisch	
9.30–9.45	—		Pause		—	
9.45–10.30	Kunst	Physik	Deutsch	Englisch	Geo	frei
10.30–11.15	Bio	Geschichte	Deutsch	Physik	Kunst	
11.15–11.30	—		Pause		—	
11.30–12.15	Musik	Sport	Bio	Geschichte	Deutsch	
12.15–13.00	—	Sport	—	Deutsch	—	

FACH/ABKÜRZUNG		NOTEN
DEUTSCH	D	1- 1 2+ 1
ENGLISCH	E	2+ 3 4+ 1- 2 2
FRANZÖSISCH	F	
LATEIN	L	3 2- 3+ 4 2+
GRIECHISCH	Gr	
MATHEMATIK	M	1 2+ 2 3- 2
PHYSIK	Ph	4 2 3

(continued on next page)

1. What is Peter's best subject? _____

2. You want to mail a letter. At what time is there a pick-up on Saturday? _____

3. You would like to know the weather forecast. What number do you call? _____

4. On what days does Peter have biology? _____

5. Does Peter have school on Saturday? _____

6. Peter is taking the train at 9:09 from Stuttgart to Düsseldorf. What time does he arrive in

   Düsseldorf? _____

7. Your cousin loves sports and knows a lot about athletes. Pick out a book for his birthday.

   _____

8. You need a new notebook and a pen for school. Where can you buy these things?

   _____

SCORE ☐

B. Petra is talking to her friend Monika on the phone. Here is their conversation, but it is out of order. Put it into the correct order by numbering the sentences in a logical sequence.
18 points

_____ Hier Monika Meier.

_____ Ja, gern.

_____ Ja, grüss dich, Monika! Hier ist Petra. Du, Monika, kennst du meine Kusine, die Annette?

_____ Nein, ich kenne sie nicht.

_____ Toll! Dann lernst du die Annette auch kennen. Sie ist sehr nett und lustig.

_____ Wirklich? Sie kommt heute mit der Bahn aus München. Meine Mutter und ich holen sie ab.
   Am Freitag haben wir eine Party. Kommst du?

SCORE ☐

C. Read the following paragraph about the student Andreas Hoffmann. Then read the statements that follow and determine whether they are true or not. Place a check mark in the appropriate column.
‹18 points

Andreas ist gut in Sport. Er spielt dreimal in der Woche Tennis, und am Wochenende spielt er immer Fussball. Im Sommer möchte er Wasserschilaufen lernen. Sein Onkel und seine Tante haben ein Haus am Tegernsee. Andreas und seine Eltern besuchen sie immer dort. Der Sportlehrer von Andreas' Schule gibt im Sommer Wassersportkurse am Tegernsee. Das findet Andreas toll!

	stimmt	stimmt nicht
1. Andreas macht gern Sport.		
2. Er spielt aber nie Fussball.		
3. Seine Eltern haben ein Haus am Tegernsee.		
4. Andreas möchte im Sommer Wasserschilaufen lernen.		
5. Andreas' Vater ist Sportlehrer.		
6. Andreas kann vielleicht im Sommer einen Kurs im Wasserschilaufen mit dem Sportlehrer von seiner Schule machen.		

SCORE ☐

D. Here are some postcards written by German students on vacation. Read what they have written and the incomplete statements that follow. Decide which of the lettered answer choices best completes each statement. Circle the letter of your choice.
20 points

Liebe Eltern!

Österreich ist toll! Wir laufen jeden Tag Schi. Onkel Franz ist wirklich sehr lustig! Kommt Ihr am Wochenende wie verabredet?

Tschüs, bis bald!
Euer Ulli

Hallo Karin!

Grüss Dich! Ich bin schon zwei Wochen bei meinem Onkel in New York und finde Englisch gar nicht schwer! Die Amerikaner sind toll! Mein Vetter Robert ist sehr nett, und wir haben viel Spass zusammen.

Dein Freund
Erich

Liebe Frau Schmidt!

Viele Grüsse aus Hamburg! Wir machen Ferien hier in Norddeutschland. Hamburg ist interessant, und wir möchten auch die Stadt Bremen besuchen. Ich hoffe, Sie haben auch einen schönen Sommer!

Ihre Schülerin
Trixi Clausen

(continued on next page)

1. Ulli schreibt an _____.

   a. seine Freundin

   b. seine Mutter und seinen Vater

   c. seinen Lehrer

2. Erich schreibt an _____.

   a. seine Schwester

   b. seine Tante

   c. seine Freundin

3. Frau Schmidt ist eine _____.

   a. Verkäuferin

   b. Polizistin

   c. Lehrerin

4. Ulli ist _____.

   a. in Deutschland

   b. in Österreich

   c. in der Schweiz

5. Ulli schreibt im _____.

   a. Sommer

   b. Winter

   c. Herbst

6. Ullis Eltern sind _____.

   a. auch da

   b. nicht da

7. Erich ist in _____.

   a. Deutschland

   b. Österreich

   c. Amerika

8. Erich und Robert sind _____.

   a. Vettern

   b. Brüder

   c. Freunde

9. Trixi macht Ferien in _____.

   a. Amerika

   b. Deutschland

   c. Österreich

10. Die Stadt Bremen ist _____.

    a. in Norddeutschland

    b. in der Schweiz

    c. in England

SCORE

A. Your mother is helping you check if you have various items you need for your trip to Germany. She reads off the list on the left, asking you if you have each item. You respond, using pronouns. Complete the questions and responses.
16 points

MUTTER: DU:

Kamera
Pass
Flugticket
Reiseschecks

1. Hast du _____? Ja, ich habe _____.

2. Hast du _____? Ja, ich habe _____.

3. Hast du _____? Ja, ich habe _____.

4. Hast du _____? Ja, ich habe _____.

SCORE [   ]

B. There is a German exchange student in your school. You are interviewing him for your school newspaper. Write five questions you could ask him to elicit the information listed below.
10 points

Name: Klaus Bachmann

Alter: 15

macht gern: Fussball, Schwimmen, Briefmarkensammeln

macht nicht gern: Gymnastik

Schulweg: Bus

1. _____

2. _____

3. _____

4. _____

5. _____

SCORE [   ]

C. Write a brief article about Klaus Bachmann, using the information given in the preceding question. The article is started for you.
10 points

Der Schüler aus Deutschland _____ Klaus Bachmann. Er _____

_____

_____

_____

_____

SCORE _____

D. Now Klaus introduces himself to your class and tells the above information about himself. Write what he says.
10 points

Ich _____ Klaus Bachmann. Ich _____

_____

_____

_____

_____

SCORE _____

E. Pretend you are an exchange student in Germany. You have been asked to tell a little about yourself. Prepare what you are going to say and write out your talk. Start out, of course, with your name and age and where you are from. Name the school you attend and some of your subjects, mentioning the ones you like the most and telling which subjects you are good in and not so good in. Also tell about some of your sports and activities.
11 points

_____

_____

_____

_____

_____

_____

_____

_____

_____

_____

_____

SCORE _____

F. Write what you would say in the following situations.
13 points

1. You are coming to school and see teachers and classmates.

   a. You greet your German teacher.

   _____

   b. You greet a friend.

   _____

2. You and your friends are discussing grades.

   a. Your friend failed the German test.

   _____

   b. Another friend got an A.

   _____

(continued on next page)

3. You and your friends are discussing school and activities.

   a. One friend thinks German is great; you agree.

   _____

   b. Another friend thinks math is hard; you disagree.

   _____

   c. You tell your friends you like to play cards.

   _____

   d. You say you prefer chess.

   _____

   e. You say you don't like tennis.

   _____

4. You are visiting a friend.

   a. Your friend shows you around the house. You like the house and express admiration for it.

   _____

   b. Your friend responds to your compliment. What does he or she say?

   _____

   c. Your friend gives you a present. You say thank you.

   _____

   d. Your friend responds to your thanks; what does he or she say?

   _____

SCORE ☐

PART FOUR Culture (optional)

Maximum Score: 40 extra points

A. Name the five German-speaking countries.
10 points

1. _____   4. _____

2. _____   5. _____

3. _____

SCORE [   ]

B. As an exchange student in Germany, you would notice similarities and differences in the way things are done in your own country and the way they are done in Germany. How observant are you? Circle the most appropriate completion to each of the following statements.
30 points

1. When you meet people, it is customary to _____.

   a. wave

   b. shake hands

   c. bow or curtsy

2. It is appropriate to greet your teacher in German with _____!

   a. Grüss dich

   b. Tschüs

   c. Guten Tag

3. You address most adults outside your family with _____.

   a. Sie

   b. du

   c. ihr

4. Most German numerals look about the same as English numerals, with the exception of _____.

   a. 3 and 8

   b. 4 and 5

   c. 1 and 7

(continued on next page)

5. When you attend a German school, you _____.

    a. buy your lunch in school

    b. bring your lunch

    c. go home for lunch

6. You enjoy sports, so you will probably join _____.

    a. a **Sportverein** outside of school

    b. one of the many school teams

    c. a hobby club, since there are no organized sports in Germany

7. If you are looking for a post office or a mailbox, it helps to know that the postal color is _____.

    a. blue

    b. yellow

    c. green

8. When traveling in Germany and many other countries, you have to be familiar with the 24-hour system of telling time. For example, you must know that **15 Uhr** is _____.

    a. 1:15 A.M.

    b. 3:00 A.M.

    c. 3:00 P.M.

9. If someone compliments you, it is appropriate for you to say _____

    a. Danke!

    b. Wirklich? Findest du?

    c. Das finde ich auch.

10. Lufthansa is a German _____.

    a. airline

    b. beer

    c. city

(continued on next page)

11. The largest airport in the BRD is in _____.

    a. Wien

    b. Dresden

    c. Frankfurt

12. **Fussball** is the game Americans call _____.

    a. football

    b. soccer

    c. lacrosse

13. In Germany, as in many European countries, distance is measured in _____.

    a. miles

    b. kilometers

    c. centimeters

14. If you want to make a call to another country from a German phone booth, you must call from a booth that has a sign reading _____.

    a. Ortsgespräch

    b. Telefon

    c. Inland/Ausland

15. To make a long-distance call, you need to know the _____.

    a. Vorwahlnummer

    b. Postleitzahl

    c. Devisenkurs

SCORE

UNIT 7 TEST

PART ONE Listening

Maximum Score: 35 points

A. You are going shopping for your mother. Listen as she tells you what to buy. Write
the number of the sentence under the picture of the grocery or other food item
mentioned in that sentence.
10 points

_____

_____

_____

_____

_____

_____

_____

_____

_____

_____

SCORE [   ]

B. Listen to the following comments. Do they express pleasure or enthusiasm, or do they express annoyance? Place a check mark in the appropriate row.
5 points

	1	2	3	4	5
pleasure/enthusiasm					
annoyance					

SCORE [ ]

C. You are listening to weather reports on the radio. Decide whether the comment that follows each report is an appropriate response or not. Place a check mark in the appropriate row.
5 points

	1	2	3	4	5
appropriate					
not appropriate					

SCORE [ ]

D. Listen to the following fragments of conversation. Is the speaker asking a question or making a request or suggestion? Place a check mark in the appropriate row.
10 points

	1	2	3	4	5	6	7	8	9	10
question										
request/suggestion										

SCORE [ ]

E. Complete the shopping list below according to what you hear. Fill in the blanks with the appropriate numbers and food items. Use numerals, not words, for the numbers.
5 points

_____ Fl. _____

_____ l _____

_____ kg _____

_____ Pfd. _____

_____ g _____

SCORE [   ]

PART TWO   Reading

Maximum Score: 20 points

A. Where should these people go? Each of the following statements is incomplete. Decide which of the lettered answer choices best completes each statement. Write the letter of your choice in the space provided.
6 points

a. beim Bäcker   d. den Supermarkt
b. beim Metzger   e. eine Imbiss-Stube
c. den Marienplatz   f. zum Gemüsehändler

_____ 1. Flori ist in München und möchte das Rathaus sehen. Er sucht _____.

_____ 2. Steffi und Flori sind in der Stadt. Sie haben Hunger und möchten eine Münchner

Spezialität, den Leberkäs, probieren. Sie gehen in _____.

_____ 3. Frau Huber braucht Butter, Zucker, Eier und Kaffee. Flori geht für sie einkaufen. Er

sucht _____.

_____ 4. Frau Huber möchte frische Semmeln haben und auch ein Brot. Sie holt das _____.

_____ 5. Frau Huber sagt: „Heute essen wir Aufschnitt und vielleicht auch Bratwurst. Ich kaufe

das immer _____."

_____ 6. „Salat, Gurken und Tomaten, und wenn sie schön sind, auch Kirschen. Steffi, geh

doch _____!"

SCORE [   ]

HBJ material copyrighted under notice appearing earlier in this work.

UNIT 7 TEST   **137**

B. There is a line missing from each of the following dialogs. The missing lines are listed below. Read each dialog and decide which of the lettered answer choices best completes it. Write the letter of your choice in the space provided.
9 points

a. Entschuldigung! Wissen Sie, wo der Chinesische Turm ist?
b. Es ist ein Dorf, ein Vorort von Bern.
c. Ich kenne die Stadt nicht.
d. Isst du noch eine Bratwurst, oder hast du genug?
e. Ja, denn nehme ich zwei Pfund, bitte!
f. Ja, probieren Sie ihn mal!
g. Keine Ahnung! Frag mal die Mutti!
h. Schau mal, die Kirschen sehen prima aus!
i. Wo ist das Glockenspiel?

1. A: Der Leberkäs ist heute sehr gut.

   B: Wirklich?

   A: _____

2. A: München ist schön und interessant.

   B: _____

   A: Dann besuch sie doch mal!

3. A: Du, Steffi, was essen wir heute?

   B: _____

   A: Frau Huber, was essen wir denn heute?

4. A: _____

   B: Ja, im Englischen Garten.

   A: Vielen Dank!

5. A: _____

   B: Sie schmeckt prima. Ich esse noch eine.

   A: Ich auch.

6. A: Was kosten die Tomaten?

   B: Ein Pfund kostet DM 2,00.

   A: _____

7. A: _____

   B: Kaufst du ein Pfund?

   A: Nein, ich habe nicht genug Geld.

8. A: Wo wohnt Bruno Schmidlin?

   B: In der Schweiz, im Zimmerwald.

   A: Ist Zimmerwald gross?

   B: _____

9. A: Und hier ist der Marienplatz und das Neue Rathaus.

   B: _____

   A: Schau, dort oben!

SCORE ⬚

C. Read the following paragraph about Germany and the city of Munich. Then read the statements below it. If a statement is true, place a check mark in the column labeled *stimmt*. If the statement is not true, place a check mark in the column labeled *stimmt nicht*.
5 points

    Die Bundesrepublik Deutschland hat elf Länder. Schleswig-Holstein ist in Norddeutschland, Bayern ist in Süddeutschland. Die Stadt Bonn am Rhein ist die Hauptstadt von Deutschland, aber viele Leute besuchen lieber die Hauptstadt von Bayern, die Stadt München. München ist eine Grossstadt — sie hat 1,3 Millionen Einwohner. Aber für die Einwohner und für die vielen Touristen ist München ein grosses Dorf — nett, gemütlich, lustig, interessant. Was siehst du alles in München? Kennst du die Sehenswürdigkeiten? Die Peterskirche ist ein Wahrzeichen von München, und das Münchner Kindl ist das offizielle Wappen. In der Innenstadt ist die Fussgängerzone, und da siehst du auch den Dom. Möchtest du in die Oper gehen? Hier ist das Nationaltheater. Oder vielleicht möchtest du ein Museum besuchen — die alte Pinakothek ist ein prima Museum! Am Marienplatz siehst du das Neue Rathaus, und im Englischen Garten steht der schöne Chinesische Turm. München hat alles — Kirchen, Schlösser, Museen, Theater. Und wann besuchst du München?

	stimmt	stimmt nicht
1. Schleswig-Holstein und Bayern sind Länder in der Bundesrepublik.		
2. Bonn ist die Hauptstadt von Bayern.		
3. München ist nicht gross.		
4. Die Peterskirche, der Dom und der Marienplatz sind Sehenswürdigkeiten von München.		
5. Du gehst in die Alte Pinakothek, wenn du eine Oper hören möchtest.		

SCORE

PART THREE Writing

Maximum Score: 45 points

A. Florian is in Munich and would like to go to the Alte Pinakothek. He is asking for directions. Complete the paragraph by filling in each blank with the correct form of **wissen.**
7 points

Hier ist ein Junge. Ich frage ihn. „Verzeihung! _____ du vielleicht, wo
(1)

die Alte Pinakothek ist?" — „Nein, das _____ ich leider nicht."
(2)

Hm, dann frage ich die Frau dort drüben. „_____ Sie, wo die
(3)

Alte Pinakothek ist, bitte?" — „Keine Ahnung." Ja, sie _____ es auch
(4)

nicht! — Moment mal, die zwei Mädchen _____ das vielleicht.
(5)

„Entschuldigung! _____ ihr, wo die Alte Pinakothek ist?" — „Na, klar!
(6)

Wir _____ das gut! Wir wohnen hier in München!" Gott sei dank!
(7)

SCORE _____

B. Steffi has plans for the day, but it looks as if they aren't going to work out. Complete the dialog by filling in each blank with a form of **sollen.**
6 points

MUTTER   Du, Steffi, _____ du heute nicht in die Stadt gehen und deinen Pass
(1)

holen?

STEFFI   Stimmt! Aber es _____ regnen, und da bleib' ich lieber da.
(2)

MUTTER   Prima! Möchtest du dann nicht für mich einkaufen gehen? Der Flori geht mit.

STEFFI   Ja, was _____ wir kaufen?
(3)

MUTTER   Hier ist der Zettel und das Geld. Und ihr _____ aufpassen und das
(4)

Geld nicht verlieren!

STEFFI   Hm, wo _____ ich die Tomaten kaufen?
(5)

MUTTER   Bei Herrn Grün. Der Flori _____ mal den Gemüsehändler
(6)

kennenlernen.

SCORE _____

140   UNIT 7 TEST

HBJ material copyrighted under notice appearing earlier in this work.

C. Frau Huber joins Steffi and Florian for lunch. They go to a little restaurant.
Complete the dialog by filling in each blank with the correct form of **essen**.
7 points

FRAU HUBER   Was sollen wir _____(1)? Alles sieht so gut aus.

FLORIAN   Ich _____(2) alles, nur nicht Leberkäs mit Senf!

STEFFI   Dann _____(3) doch zwei Weisswürste! Sie sind eine Münchner
Spezialität.

FRAU HUBER   Na gut! Was _____(4) ihr nun? _____(5) du
Weisswürste, Flori?

FLORIAN   Ja, und die Steffi _____(6) eine Bratwurst. Was

_____(7) Sie?

SCORE [ ]

FRAU HUBER   Hm, ich möchte den Leberkäs probieren.

D. Write how you would make the following requests and suggestions to the people mentioned.
7 points

1. Monika, eine Klassenkameradin, soll den Lehrer fragen.

_____

2. Frank, dein Freund, soll Frau Meier das Buch zeigen.

_____

3. Herr Schmidt, der Deutschlehrer, soll mal die Stadt München besuchen.

_____

4. Hans und Sabine, deine Geschwister, sollen die Spielkarten nicht verlieren.

_____

5. Deine Mutter soll mal eine Pizza essen.

_____

6. Dein Vater soll das Hähnchen probieren.

_____

7. Deine Freunde sollen zu Hause bleiben.

_____

SCORE [ ]

E. You are new in Munich and want to get to the National Theater. The first person you ask for directions doesn't know. The second person tells you it's on the Maximilianstrasse. Write the dialog.
6 points

Du   _____
                              (1)

Mann   _____
                              (2)

Du   _____
                              (3)

Du   _____
                              (4)

Mädchen _____
                              (5)

Du   _____
                              (6)

SCORE [   ]

F. You and a friend are in a restaurant. Your friend is having **Bratwurst** and you are having **Leberkäs.** Ask each other how the food tastes and respond appropriately. Then the waiter comes and asks each of you if you want more. Respond appropriately. Write the dialog.
8 points

Du   _____
                              (1)

Freund _____
                              (2)

        _____
                              (3)

Du   _____
                              (4)

Kellner _____
                              (5)

Freund _____
                              (6)

Kellner _____
                              (7)

Du   _____
                              (8)

SCORE [   ]

G. Your mother asks you to go shopping. Write a dialog between your mother and you of at least four lines. Here is a list of the things she needs:

1 kg Tomaten

2 Pfd. Zucker

10 Eier

4 points   6 Semmeln

_____

_____

_____

_____

_____

SCORE ⬚

PART FOUR Culture (optional)

Maximum Score: 5 extra points

Circle the letter of the correct completion to each statement.
5 points

1. Das deutsche Pfund hat _____ Gramm.

   a. 100

   b. 250

   c. 500

2. Die Hauptstadt der BRD heisst _____.

   a. Berlin

   b. Bonn

   c. München

3. Schleswig-Holstein ist _____.

   a. eine Stadt

   b. ein Land

   c. ein Dorf

4. Die Alte Pinakothek ist _____.

   a. ein Museum

   b. eine Kirche

   c. ein Schloss

5. „Gruetzi" hörst du meistens _____.

   a. in Nordrhein-Westfalen

   b. in Bayern

   c. in der Schweiz

SCORE ⬚

HBJ material copyrighted under notice appearing earlier in this work.

UNIT 7 TEST   **143**

REVIEW TEST 2 • Units 5–8

PART ONE Listening

Maximum Score: 50 points

A. Peter Seber is packing for his trip to Germany. You will hear him or some member of his family mention various items. Decide which items he would logically take along on his trip and which ones he would leave home. Place a check mark in the appropriate row.
8 points

	1	2	3	4	5	6	7	8
braucht								
braucht nicht								

SCORE ☐

B. What are you listening to? Is it a flight announcement at the airport or a weather report on the radio? Is someone making an introduction, giving directions, or describing someone? Listen carefully, determine which it is, and place a check mark in the appropriate row.
10 points

	1	2	3	4	5
flight announcement					
weather report					
introduction					
directions					
description					

SCORE ☐

C. Listen to the following fragments of conversation. Where is each conversation taking place? Write the number of the conversation next to the most logical location.
20 points

_____ beim Bäcker   _____ beim Metzger

_____ in der Bank   _____ in München

_____ im Flughafen an der Passkontrolle   _____ in der Post

_____ im Geschenkladen   _____ im Supermarkt

_____ in der Imbiss-Stube   _____ am Telefon

SCORE [   ]

D. You will hear one person ask for directions and another person reply. Check against the street map below to find out whether the second person's directions are accurate or not. Place a check mark in the appropriate row.
12 points

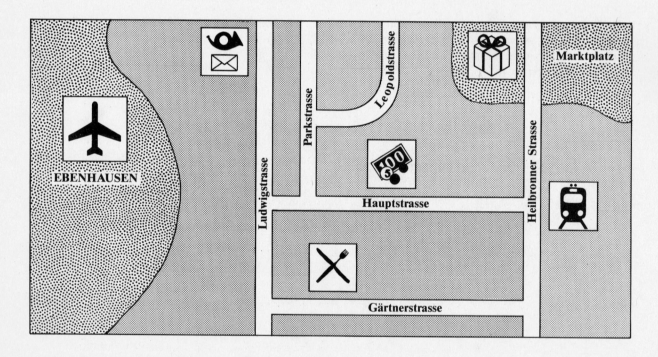

	1	2	3	4	5	6
stimmt						
stimmt nicht						

SCORE [   ]

146   REVIEW TEST 2

PART TWO Reading

Maximum Score: 30 points

A. The pictures below are followed by descriptions. Read each description and match it with the picture. Write the number of the picture in the space provided.
10 points

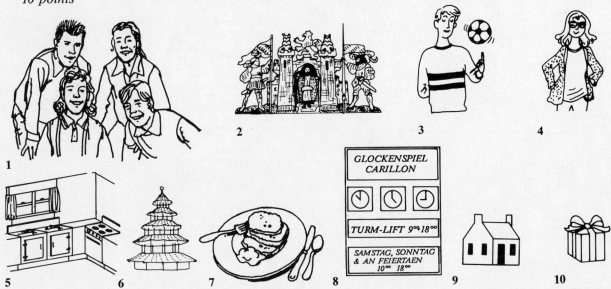

1   2   3   4

5   6   7   8   9   10

_____ Es ist in München, am Marienplatz, oben im Rathaus. Du stehst unten, und um 11 Uhr hörst du es, und du kannst sehen, wie die Figuren sich bewegen.

_____ Es sieht sehr schön aus. Klein und interessant. Was ist es? Für wen ist es?

_____ Er ist gross und schlank, hört gern Musik und spielt Fussball.

_____ Sie sind nett und lustig. Wenn wir eine Party haben, macht es immer viel Spass. Ich finde sie alle sehr sympathisch.

_____ Du findest ihn im Englischen Garten. Er ist ein Wahrzeichen Münchens. Er sieht nicht sehr deutsch aus, aber er ist schön!

_____ Sie ist modern und sehr praktisch. Auch sehr hell. Sie ist aber klein, und wir essen immer im Esszimmer.

_____ Sie ist intelligent, freundlich, hat eine Brille. Sie hat viele Freunde. Sie spielt Gitarre und macht auch gern Sport.

_____ Es ist hübsch und gemütlich. Es hat sechs Zimmer, einen tollen Partykeller und einen schönen Garten.

_____ Es ist das offizielle Wappen von München. Es ist ein kleiner Mönch. In der Hand hält er einen Bierkrug. Die Mönche haben im Mittelalter die Bierbrauerei gegründet.

_____ Mit Senf schmeckt er prima. Er ist heiss und frisch und kostet auch nicht viel. Probier doch mal! Oder bist du satt?

SCORE [____]

HBJ material copyrighted under notice appearing earlier in this work.

REVIEW TEST 2   **147**

B. Peter has been in Germany for two weeks, and his German has been improving rapidly. Here are some of the many things he has had to read and understand. Can you read and understand them too? Answer the questions that follow.

20 points

Wie ist das Wetter in Deutschland?

heiter
bewölkt
Regen

Deutscher Kopfsalat	Stck.	–.39
Spanische Tomaten	1 kg	4.00
Hohes C Orangensaft	0,7 l	1.69
Jakobs Kaffee	500 g	10,60
Deutsche Markenbutter	250 g	2,20
Joghurt, natur	150 g	–,49
Deutscher Tilsiter	100 g	–,79

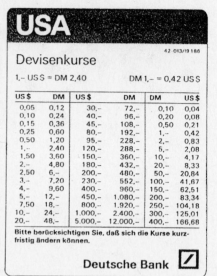

USA

42-013/19 186

Devisenkurse

1.– US $ = DM 2,40   DM 1,– = 0,42 US $

US $	DM	US $	DM	DM	US $
0,05	0,12	30,–	72,–	0,10	0,04
0,10	0,24	40,–	96,–	0,20	0,08
0,15	0,36	45,–	108,–	0,50	0,21
0,25	0,60	80,–	192,–	1,–	0,42
0,50	1,20	95,–	228,–	2,–	0,83
1,–	2,40	120,–	288,–	5,–	2,08
1,50	3,60	150,–	360,–	10,–	4,17
2,–	4,80	180,–	432,–	20,–	8,33
2,50	6,–	200,–	480,–	50,–	20,84
3,–	7,20	230,–	552,–	100,–	41,67
4,–	9,60	400,–	960,–	150,–	62,51
5,–	12,–	450,–	1.080,–	200,–	83,34
7,50	18,–	800,–	1.920,–	250,–	104,18
10,–	24,–	1.000,–	2.400,–	300,–	125,01
20,–	48,–	5.000,–	12.000,–	400,–	166,68

Bitte berücksichtigen Sie, daß sich die Kurse kurzfristig ändern können.

Deutsche Bank ◪

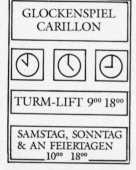

GLOCKENSPIEL
CARILLON

TURM-LIFT 9⁰⁰ 18⁰⁰

SAMSTAG, SONNTAG
& AN FEIERTAGEN
10⁰⁰ 18⁰⁰

DB Deutsche Bundesbahn					
Station	**Uhr**	**Uhr**	**Uhr**	**Uhr**	**Uhr**
Köln ab	7.08	8.20	9.30	10.10	17.00
München an	12.00	13.10	14.15	15.36	22.56

Inlandsgespräche - Auslandsgespräche

1	2	3	Angezeigter Betrag kann durch Drücken der grünen Taste für weitere Gespräche genutzt werden.	4
	Minimum DM 0,20			

Polizei Police	110		11 88	Standort - Nr. 75 M 011	Störung 1171 münzfrei
	112	✚ 222 666	0 01 18	Standort Kemptener - Allgauer - Str.	
				Ortsnetz München	

Keine Telegramme, keine handvermittelten Gespräche, keine Rückgabe des Restbetrages von 1-DM- und 5-DM-Münzen

NEUES RATHAUS
erbaut von
Georg von Hauberrisser
In den Jahren 1867–1908

1 Kg Tomaten
250 g Kaffee
125 g Butter
1 l Milch
375 g Aufschnitt
500 g Hackfleisch

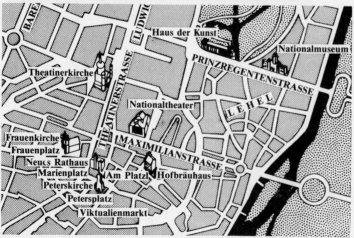

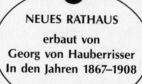

IMBISS

Leberkäs	3,50
Wurstbrot	2,40
Fischbrot	3,50
Pizza	6,00
Mineralwasser	1,80
Cola	2,60
Kaffee	2,40

1. Peter ist in München zu Besuch. Er will telefonieren, aber er braucht erst Information. Welche

   Nummer muss er wählen? _____

2. Er möchte Geld wechseln. Wie ist der Kurs? _____

3. Peter und Wiebke gehen für Frau Nedel einkaufen. Was holen sie alles im Supermarkt? _____

   _____

   _____

4. Was kostet ein Pfund Kaffee? _____

5. Peter möchte Freunde in München besuchen. In der Zeitung liest er den Wetterbericht für

   München. Wie soll das Wetter sein? _____

   _____

6. Peter kommt mit der Bahn nach München. Der Zug geht um 9.30 von Köln ab. Wann ist Peter in

   München? _____

7. Peter ist in der Stadt. Er probiert eine Münchner Spezialität. Was isst er? _____

   _____

8. Wo ist das Nationalmuseum? _____

9. Wer hat das Neue Rathaus gebaut? _____

10. Wann kann Peter das Glockenspiel im Neuen Rathaus sehen und hören? _____

   _____

SCORE [   ]

PART THREE Writing

A. You are at the information desk in the airport and want to know where the following places are: the bank, the telephone, and the gift shop. Using the diagram below, write your questions and the information clerk's responses.
6 points

1. A: _____

   B: _____

2. A: _____

   B: _____

3. A: _____

   B: _____

SCORE [   ]

B. You are shopping and decide you need another one of each of the following items. Write what you say.
5 points

1. Ich brauche _____ Brot.

2. Ich brauche _____ Flasche Mineralwasser.

3. Ich brauche _____ Kopf Salat.

4. Ich brauche _____ Pfund Butter.

5. Ich brauche _____ 200 Gramm Käse.

SCORE
[   ]

C. Your mother asks you to go shopping. You're supposed to buy the items on the shopping list to the left. She tells you where. Choose the appropriate place of business from the second list and write your mother's requests. Use the verbs **kaufen** and **holen** and words such as **bitte, doch,** or **mal.**
5 points

Kirschen
Aufschnitt
Semmeln
Zucker
Briefmarken

1. _____

2. _____

3. _____

in der Post

beim Bäcker

beim Gemüsehändler

beim Metzger

im Supermarkt

4. _____

5. _____

SCORE _____

D. You and your friends are going out. Your father is giving you some last-minute instructions. Using the command form, write what he says.
3 points

1. Ihr sollt nicht zu spät nach Hause kommen.

_____

2. Ihr sollt das Geld nicht verlieren.

_____

3. Ihr sollt nicht zu viel essen.

_____

SCORE _____

E. Frau Schneider and Flori are checking the gifts Flori will take to the Hubers in Munich. Complete the dialog by filling in each blank with an appropriate word from the list. *5 points*

die — die — den — ein — eine — einen — Herrn — ihn — sie — wen

FRAU SCHNEIDER Für _____ ist die Halskette?
(1)

FLORI Sie ist für _____ Steffi.
(2)

FRAU SCHNEIDER Was hast du für Steffis Vater?

FLORI Für _____ Huber? Für _____ habe ich
(3)   (4)

_____ Taschenrechner.
(5)

FRAU SCHNEIDER Und für Steffis Geschwister? Was hast du für _____?
(6)

FLORI Für _____ Anni habe ich _____ Buch, und
(7)   (8)

für _____ Markus habe ich _____ Musikkassette.
(9)   (10)

SCORE [ ]

F. Flori has never visited the Hubers before, and Steffi shows him around the apartment. Write what she says as she shows him around. Flori likes the apartment. What does he say? How does Steffi respond? *9 points*

STEFFI Wir haben sechs Zimmer. Wir haben _____ und
(1)

_____. Hier ist _____. Wir haben drei
(2)   (3)

_____. Hier ist _____ für die Eltern,
(4)   (5)

und hier ist _____. Wir haben auch _____.
(6)   (7)
Das ist jetzt dein Zimmer.

FLORI _____
(8)

STEFFI _____
(9)

SCORE [ ]

G. Steffi and Flori go to a party at Renate Baumann's house. Renate is a good friend of Steffi's. Steffi introduces Flori to Renate, and Renate introduces her mother and her father. Write what Steffi and Renate say in each case and what Flori says.
10 points

STEFFI _____
(1)

RENATE _____
(2)

STEFFI _____
(3)

FLORI _____
(4)

RENATE _____
(5)

FLORI _____
(6)

Then Renate's brother Bernd and a classmate, Sylvie, introduce themselves. Write what they say and what Flori says.

BERND _____
(7)

FLORI _____
(8)

SYLVIE _____
(9)

FLORI _____
(10)

SCORE ☐

H. Flori and Steffi are about to leave to go sightseeing. Use a definite article to complete what Frau Huber says. Use a pronoun to complete what Steffi says.
8 points

FRAU HUBER: STEFFI:

1. Hast du _____ Geld?   Ja, ich habe _____.

2. Hast du _____ Regenschirme? Ja, ich habe _____.

3. Hast du _____ Kamera?   Ja, ich habe _____.

4. Hast du _____ Reiseführer? Ja, ich habe _____.

SCORE ☐

I. In Munich Flori distributes the gifts. Steffi thanks Flori and Flori makes a suitable reply. Complete the dialog.
2 points

FLORI Hier ist eine Halskette für Steffi.

STEFFI _____
         (1)

FLORI _____
         (2)

J. Flori gets hungry as he and Steffi are sightseeing. They meet Steffi's friend Renate and go to get something to eat. Complete the dialog by filling in each blank with the correct form of an appropriate verb from the boxed list.
8 points

> aussehen — essen — wissen — sollen

FLORI _____ du, wo eine Imbiss-Stube ist? Ich habe Hunger und möchte
       (1)

  etwas _____ .
     (2)

STEFFI Dort drüben ist eine Imbiss-Stube. Sie _____ gut _____ .
            (3)   (4)

  Was _____ du lieber? Leberkäs? Pizza?
     (5)

FLORI Ich _____ nicht. Ich _____ wirklich alles gern.
     (6)   (7)

STEFFI Du _____ mal den Leberkäs probieren. Aber die Bratwurst und die
     (8)

  Pizza _____ auch gut _____ .
      (9)   (10)

RENATE _____ ihr nicht, was ihr _____ wollt? Was
     (11)   (12)

  _____ ihr gern? Frag mal den Kellner, was heute gut ist!
     (13)

KELLNER Sie möchten?

STEFFI Was ist heute gut? _____ wir Pizza oder Leberkäs
         (14)

  _____ ?
    (15)

KELLNER Tja, was _____ Sie gern? Alles, was wir haben,
       (16)

  schmeckt gut!

K. You are in Munich. Flori asks you for directions to the **Nationalmuseum,** but you don't know where it is. Flori then asks a man passing by, who tells him the **Nationalmuseum** is on Prinzregenten Street. Write the dialogs.
4 points

FLORI _____
(1)

DU _____
(2)

FLORI _____
(3)

MANN _____
(4)

SCORE [   ]

L. Here is some information about Steffi Huber. Write how she introduces herself and tells you about where she lives. Then, in the same format, write information about yourself or someone you know and write a similar paragraph.
5 points

Steffi Huber / München, Hauptstadt von Bayern / 1,3 Millionen Einwohner

1. Grüss Gott! Ich bin _____

_____

_____

2. _____

_____

_____

SCORE [   ]

Do you know where the states are located in the Federal Republic? For only ten of the eleven **Bundesländer,** write the letter of the state next to its name in the space provided.
10 points

_____ 1. Baden-Württemberg

_____ 2. Bayern

_____ 3. Berlin (West)

_____ 4. Bremen

_____ 5. Hamburg

_____ 6. Hessen

_____ 7. Niedersachsen

_____ 8. Nordrhein-Westfalen

_____ 9. Rheinland-Pfalz

_____ 10. Saarland

_____ 11. Schleswig-Holstein

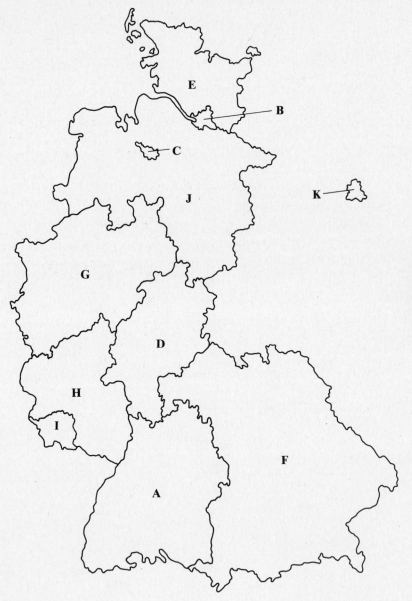

SCORE

UNIT 9 TEST

PART ONE Listening

Maximum Score: 30 points

A. Here is part of Karin's party guest list. Listen as she invites her friends. Who's coming and who isn't? Place a check mark in the appropriate column.
5 points

	kommt	kommt nicht
Hans-Peter		
Michaela		
Brigitte		
Klaus		
Bernd		

SCORE [   ]

B. Karin is telling her friend Christine about the party. Listen to what Karin says; what is she talking about? Place a check mark in the appropriate row.
10 points

	1	2	3	4	5
who's coming					
who's not coming					
what there is to eat					
what there is to drink					
what they'll do at the party					

SCORE [   ]

C. At Karin's party you overhear fragments of conversation. Decide what the people are talking about: are they extending an invitation? Offering something to eat or to drink? Paying a compliment? Place a check mark in the appropriate row.
10 points

	1	2	3	4	5	6	7	8	9	10
inviting										
offering										
complimenting										

SCORE [   ]

D. Listen to the following exchanges Decide whether the response to each question or comment is appropriate or not and place a check mark in the appropriate row.
5 points

	1	2	3	4	5
appropriate					
not appropriate					

SCORE [   ]

PART TWO Reading

Maximum Score: 20 points

A. Read the following invitation and answer the questions that follow.
5 points

1. Wann ist die Party? _____

2. Wo ist die Party? _____

3. Wer lädt dich ein? _____

4. Was machst du dort? _____

5. Was sollst du bringen? _____

SCORE ☐

B. Karin is writing to her friend Marlies. Read the letter and determine whether the statements below it are true or not. Place a check mark in the appropriate row.
9 points

Liebe Marlies!

     Am Samstag in zwei Wochen — am 16. Oktober — habe ich eine Party. Kommst du? Ich lade viele Freunde ein. Du kennst sie alle: Bernd, Uwe, Christine, Michaela, Hans-Peter, Matthias, Lisa und Heidi. Leider kommt die Brigitte nicht. Sie besucht ihre Tante in München. Und der Klaus hat auch etwas vor. Es gibt wie immer viel zu essen und zu trinken — Gulaschsuppe, Bratwurst und Kartoffelsalat. Ich mache Käsebrote und vielleicht auch Wurstbrote. Mein Bruder grillt für uns Hamburger, und meine Mutter macht wieder ihren tollen Kuchen. Mein Vater macht eine Erdbeerbowle. Alle trinken sie so gern. Und was noch? Ja, wir haben viele Platten und Musik-kassetten — es gibt tolle Musik! Und vielleicht spielen wir auch ein Ratespiel. Du weisst, es ist eine lustige Gruppe, und ein Ratespiel macht dann Spass!

     Ich hoffe, du kannst kommen! Ruf mich bitte an!

Bis bald!
Deine Karin

---

	stimmt	stimmt nicht
1. Karin lädt Marlies ein.		
2. Die Party ist im Herbst.		
3. Marlies kennt Karins Freunde nicht.		
4. Brigitte und Klaus kommen nicht.		
5. Karins Eltern machen nichts für die Party. Karin macht alles allein.		
6. Es gibt viel zu essen und zu trinken, aber es gibt keine Suppe.		
7. Karin findet ihre Freunde lustig.		
8. Sie findet Ratespiele langweilig.		
9. Karin weiss nicht, ob Marlies zur Party kommt.		

SCORE

C. Read the following comments and, for each one, decide which of the lettered choices below would most logically follow. Circle the letter of your choice.
6 points

1. Die Gulaschsuppe ist ausgezeichnet.

   a. Wirklich? Das freut mich.

   b. Danke.

   c. Du isst Suppe nicht gern?

2. He, Bernd, deine Kassette ist furchtbar!

   a. Möchtest du tanzen?

   b. Möchtest du sie noch einmal hören?

   c. Meinst du? Ich finde sie gut!

3. Ich trinke gern Milch.

   a. Wir haben leider keine Milch! Möchtest du einen Apfelsaft?

   b. Hier, für dich eine Limo!

   c. Möchtest du ein Wurstbrot?

4. Was machen wir jetzt? Ich möchte tanzen!

   a. Du spinnst wohl. Ich habe keinen Video-Recorder!

   b. Ja, ich auch! Wo ist die Musik?

   c. Mensch, Bernd! Deine Witze sind blöd!

5. Du, Karin, die Party ist Klasse!

   a. Schade! Es geht leider nicht.

   b. Findest du? Da bin ich aber froh!

   c. Wo sind die Platten?

6. Wann essen wir? Ich habe einen Bärenhunger!

   a. Guten Appetit!

   b. Du spinnst!

   c. Gleich!

SCORE ☐

PART THREE Writing

A. You have received the following invitations. Accept two and decline two, giving reasons where appropriate. Vary the expressions you use in your answers.
8 points

1. Eine Freundin: Ich habe am Samstag eine Party. Kommst du?

   _____

2. Zwei Klassenkameraden: Wir gehen morgen schwimmen. Kommst du?

   _____

3. Deine Tante: Am Sonntag kommt die Familie. Deine Vetter und Kusinen sind alle da. Kommst du auch?

   _____

4. Dein Freund: Ich möchte heute Tennis spielen. Möchtest du auch spielen?

   _____

SCORE ☐

B. Karin is calling up people to invite them to her party. Each person repeats the invitation to someone else. Fill in the blanks with the appropriate personal pronouns.
6 points

KARIN   Sabine, ich möchte _____ einladen.
                                          (1)

SABINE   *[zur Mutter]* Mutti, Karin möchte _____ einladen! Sie hat
               eine Party.   (2)

KARIN   Du, Michael, ist die Renate auch da? Ich möchte _____
               einladen, Samstag um acht.   (3)

MICHAEL   *[zu Renate]* He, Renate, die Karin möchte _____ einladen!
                                                              (4)

KARIN   Guten Tag, Frau Schmidt. Ich habe am Samstag eine Party, und ich möchte

               _____ und Herrn Schmidt einladen.
                      (5)

FRAU SCHMIDT   *[zu Herrn Schmidt]* Gerhard, die Karin Haupt, eine Schülerin in meiner 9b, möchte

               _____ einladen. Sollen wir gehen?
                      (6)

SCORE ☐

C. Michael and Karin are talking about whom to invite to the party. Complete the following conversation by filling in the blanks with appropriate forms of the verb **einladen.**
6 points

MICHAEL   Karin, _____ du die Brigitte _____?
                          (1a)   **(1b)**

KARIN   Ja, ich _____ sie _____. Brigitte
                          (2a)   **(2b)**

_____ mich immer _____. Sonia und Ulli
          (3a)   **(3b)**

_____ mich auch immer _____. Michael, wenn
          (4a)   **(4b)**

ihr eine Party habt, _____ ihr auch die Lehrer _____?
                                  (5a)   **(5b)**

MICHAEL   Manchmal _____ wir einen Lehrer _____.
                                  (6a)   **(6b)**

SCORE ☐

D. Karin is offering her friends something to eat at the party. Complete the following conversation by filling in each blank with an appropriate form of **nehmen.**
6 points

KARIN   Matthias, was _____ du?
                                      (1)

MATTHIAS   Hm, ich _____ eine Bratwurst.
                              (2)

KARIN   Und Christine, Michaela, was _____ ihr? Der Matthias
                                                      (3)

_____ eine Bratwurst.
          (4)

CHRISTINE   Wir _____ einen Hamburger.
                          (5)

KARIN   Frau Schmidt, _____ Sie auch einen Hamburger?
                                      (6)

FRAU SCHMIDT   Nein, danke.

SCORE ☐

E. Now Karin is offering you various things to eat and drink. Decline everything, using **kein** — but be polite.
5 points

1. Möchtest du einen Hamburger?

   _____

2. Hier, probier mal eine Bratwurst!

   _____

3. Was nimmst du? Einen Apfelsaft vielleicht?

   _____

4. Der Kuchen ist ausgezeichnet. Möchtest du ihn nicht probieren?

   _____

5. Möchtest du die Erdbeerbowle probieren? Sie schmeckt wirklich gut.

   _____

SCORE [   ]

F. At Karin's party you compliment a number of people and different things. Write the compliments and responses, using the suggestions given and using appropriate possessives.
6 points

Christine, die Musikkassetten

Du _____
                                    (1)

Christine _____
                                    (2)

Frau Haupt, der Kartoffelsalat

Du _____
                                    (3)

Frau Haupt _____
                                    (4)

Karin und ihr Bruder, das Haus

Du _____
                                    (5)

Karin _____
                                    (6)

SCORE [   ]

G. You are telling a friend about Karin's party. Complete the following paragraph by filling in each blank with the correct form of an appropriate possessive.
4 points

Karins Party ist Klasse. _____ Eltern sind nett, und
(1)

_____ Haus ist schön. _____ Freund Bernd erzählt
(2)   (3)

immer Witze. _____ Witze sind blöd, aber er ist sehr lustig.
(4)

SCORE ☐

H. Pretend you are having a party. A friend asks you some questions about it, and you reply. Write the dialog, including the following questions:

• Who are you inviting?

• What are you going to have to eat and drink?

• What are you going to do?
9 points

FREUND _____
(1)

DU _____
(2)

_____
(3)

FREUND _____
(4)

DU _____
(5)

_____
(6)

FREUND _____
(7)

DU _____
(8)

_____
(9)

SCORE ☐

Maximum Score: 5 extra points

Peter learns that quite a few things are different in Germany, but some things aren't.
Decide which of the lettered answer choices correctly completes each statement. Circle
the letter of your choice.
5 points

1. In Deutschland isst man mit der Gabel in der _____ Hand.

   a. linken

   b. rechten

2. Man sagt _____ zu einem Lehrer.

   a. „du"

   b. „Sie"

3. Die meisten Deutschen essen _____ zu Mittag.

   a. Wurstbrote oder Käsebrote

   b. ein grosses, warmes Essen

4. Wenn man in Deutschland auf eine Party geht, bringt man _____ mit.

   a. Blumen oder Schokolade

   b. nichts

5. Die Musik ist _____ als zu Hause, meint Peter.

   a. nicht viel anders

   b. viel anders

SCORE [   ]

UNIT 10 TEST

PART ONE Listening

Maximum Score: 35 points

A. You will hear some young people discussing where they want to go and what they want to do. One person makes a suggestion; another thinks it's a good idea or not such a good idea. Listen to what they say and decide which it is. Place a check mark in the appropriate row.
6 points

	1	2	3	4	5	6
gute Idee						
keine gute Idee						

SCORE ☐

B. Listen to the following people meet and greet each other. In each case, how enthusiastic or unenthusiastic is the second person's response to **Wie geht's?** Decide where it belongs on a positive-to-negative scale and write the number of the response in the appropriate space on the chart.
6 points

SCORE ☐

C. Listen to the following suggestions, each of which is missing a verb. Decide which verb from the list below correctly completes the suggestion. Write the number of the suggestion in the space provided.
8 points

_____ besuchen   _____ machen

_____ essen   _____ sehen

_____ fahren   _____ spielen

_____ hören   _____ trinken

SCORE ☐

D. Here is a page from Stefan's weekly calendar. His friend Markus calls up to arrange a date to do something together. As you hear Markus suggest a date, look at the calendar and determine whether Stefan could make it or not. Place a check mark in the appropriate row.
5 points

OKTOBER		
Mo	1900 Kegeln	**15**
Di	1400 Fussballtraining	**16**
Mi	1500 Stadtbummel mit Sabine	**17**
Do	1400 Fussballtraining	**18**
Fr		**19**
Sa	1400 Tennis mit Arnold 2000 Sabines Party	**20**
So		**21**

	1	2	3	4	5
es geht					
es geht nicht					

SCORE [ ]

E. Listen as various young people talk about what they and their friends are going to do or what they already did. Place a check mark in the appropriate row.
10 points

	1	2	3	4	5	6	7	8	9	10
going to do										
already did										

SCORE [ ]

PART TWO Reading

Maximum Score: 16 points

A. Sabine and Stefan are looking at the concert ads you see below as they discuss where to go. Complete their dialog by filling in the blanks with information from the concert ads.
10 points

STEFAN   Du, Sabine, willst du ins Kino gehen oder lieber in ein Konzert?

SABINE   Ach, Stefan, das ist mir gleich. Schauen wir mal in die Zeitung!

STEFAN   Hier, _____ .
                               (1)

SABINE   Prima! Wer singt?

STEFAN   Da ist der _____
         aus Österreich.   (2)

SABINE   Wo singt er, und wann fängt das Konzert an?

STEFAN   Moment mal! Hier, in der

         _____ um
                   (3)

         _____ .
                   (4)

KONZERTE „live"			
JAZZ	*ROCK*	*SOUL*	*ACTION*
Fr. 17.10.		CIRCUS KRONE	20.00
SALSA FESTIVAL mit Eddie Palmieri Orchestra, Salsa Picante, und Celia Cruz & Tito Puente Orchestra			
Fr. 17.10.		ALABAMAHALLE	20.30
SCORPIONS Monsters of Rock, mit Ozzy Osbourne, Bon Jovi, Warlock			
Fr. 17.10		OLYMPIAHALLE	20.00
QUEEN Die Englische Rockgruppe VORGRUPPE: Craaft – Eine deutsche Band auf dem Sprung in die US-Charts			
Sa. 18.10.		OLYMPIAHALLE	20.00
FALCO Der österreichische Popstar			
Sa. 18.10		CIRCUS KRONE	20.00
REGGAE SUNSPLASH mit Black Uhuru, The Wailers, Dennis Brown & Guests			
Sa. 18.10		ALABAMAHALLE	20.30
SUPERCHARGE Die sagenhafte Rhythm'n Blues Band			

SABINE   Aber schau, heute ist Freitag. Er singt am _____ .
                                                                (5)

STEFAN   Stimmt! Also, heute spielt die Gruppe _____ in der
                                                              (6)
         Olympiahalle. Magst du sie?

SABINE   Ja, ich höre sie gern. Was gibt es noch?

STEFAN   Es gibt im Circus Krone ein _____ , und in der Alabamahalle
                                                  (7)

         singen die _____ .
                            (8)

SABINE   Mensch, die _____ ! Das ist meine Lieblingsgruppe! Hörst du
                              (9)
         sie auch gern?

STEFAN   Ja, ich höre alle _____ gern.
                                   (10)

SABINE   Dann gehen wir in die Alabamahalle?

STEFAN   Gut, gehen wir in die Alabamahalle!

SCORE [   ]

B. You overhear some young people talking about what they do in their free time. In each case, you missed the beginning of the conversation—but you can figure out what was said! Decide which of the lettered answer choices is the correct missing first line of each speech. Write the letter in the space provided.
6 points

a. Ich mache gern Sport.

b. Meine Freundin und ich fahren oft in die Stadt.

c. Ich besuche meine Freunde.

d. Ich lese gern.

e. Am liebsten gehe ich ins Kino!

f. Wir sind eine Clique, drei Mädchen und drei Jungen.

_____ 1. Action-Filme und Komödien sehe ich gern — aber ich mag ja alle Filme!

_____ 2. Dreimal in der Woche spiele ich Tennis, am Wochenende gehe ich schwimmen und freitags mache ich immer Gymnastik.

_____ 3. Ich habe viele Bücher — Sportbücher, Hobbybücher, Fantasy-Bücher und Romane. Es ist schön, mal zu Hause zu bleiben und zu lesen.

_____ 4. Wir machen einen Stadtbummel und gehen dann in ein Café und essen ein Eis.

_____ 5. Wir hören Kassetten. Manchmal spielen wir auch Karten.

_____ 6. Wir machen viel zusammen. Wir fahren Rad, wir gehen schwimmen, wir spielen Squash und wir gehen auch mal in die Disko oder ins Kino.

SCORE _____

PART THREE   Writing

Maximum Score: 49 points

A. Here is a page torn from Sabine's calendar. Write what she did each day last week.
Use the conversational past.
6 points

APRIL		
Mo	Tennis	5
Di	Tante Anna besuchen	6
Mi	Stadtbummel mit Stefan	7
Do	Kartenspielen	8
Fr	Kino	9
Sa	Köln	10
So		11

1. _____

2. _____

3. _____

4. _____

5. _____

6. _____

SCORE ☐

B. The following questionnaire is being distributed to teenagers to find out about their likes and dislikes, but the questions are too smudged to decipher. Complete them by filling in each blank with the correct form of **welch-** or **was für ein,** as indicated. *10 points*

Was meinst du? Welch-...

1. _____ Gruppe ist deine Lieblingsgruppe?

2. _____ Sänger möchtest du am liebsten kennenlernen?

3. _____ Sängerin findest du Klasse?

4. _____ Schauspieler ist besonders lustig?

5. _____ Filme hast du in diesem Monat schon gesehen?

6. Es gibt diese Woche ein Falco-Konzert und ein Nina-Hagen-Konzert.

   _____ Konzert möchtest du lieber hören?

Was für...

7. _____ Film möchtest du am liebsten sehen?

8. _____ Konzert möchtest du am liebsten hören?

9. _____ Gruppe hörst du am liebsten?

10. _____ Sportveranstaltungen findest du uninteressant?

SCORE ☐

C. Complete the following dialog by filling in each blank with the appropriate form of
können.
6 points

A: Wir _____ heute ins Kino gehen.
  (1)

B: Ich _____ nicht.
  (2)

A: Warum _____ du nicht?
  (3)

B: Ich habe morgen eine Klassenarbeit. Der Robert auch. Er _____ auch nicht ins Kino.
  (4)

A: _____ ihr nicht nach dem Kino für die Arbeit lernen?
  (5)

B: Leider _____ meine Eltern das nicht verstehen. Sie sagen nein.
  (6)

SCORE ☐

D. Complete the following dialog by filling in each blank with the appropriate form of
wollen.
6 points

A: _____ du einen Stadtbummel machen?
  (1)

B: Ich _____ lieber Tennis spielen.
  (2)

A: Sabine und Stefan _____ aber einen Stadtbummel machen. Stefan _____
  (3)   (4)
dann auch ins Kino gehen. Ich auch.

B: Ihr _____ immer ins Kino gehen!
  (5)

A: Das stimmt! Wir _____ immer ins Kino gehen. Das machen wir gern.
  (6)

SCORE ☐

HBJ material copyrighted under notice appearing earlier in this work.

UNIT 10 TEST **173**

E. Complete the following dialog by filling in each blank with the appropriate form of **fahren.**
7 points

SABINE   Wer _____ heute in die Stadt? _____ du, Antje?
                    (1)   **(2)**

ANTJE   Ich _____ nicht. Aber vielleicht _____ Christa und Elke.
                  (3)   **(4)**
          Frag sie mal!

SABINE   Christa, Elke! _____ ihr heute in die Stadt?
                            (5)

CHRISTA   Wir _____ auch nicht. Du, Sabine, _____ doch allein!
                   (6)   **(7)**

SABINE   Das macht keinen Spass.

SCORE [   ]

F. Complete the following dialog with appropriate forms of **mögen** and **anfangen.**
7 points

A: _____ du Steve Martin?
        (1)

B: Ja, ich _____ ihn gern. Seine neue Komödie spielt jetzt im Film-Palast.
              (2)

A: Wann _____ der Film _____? Um 7?
             (3a)   **(3b)**

B: Ja. Da kommen auch Hans und Eva. He, _____ ihr Steve Martin? Wir gehen jetzt ins
                                         (4)
          Kino und sehen seinen neuen Film.

C: Stefan _____ ihn gern. Aber wir _____ Robin Williams lieber. Sein
                  (5)   **(6)**

          neuer Film spielt auch jetzt in der Stadt. Ich glaube, die zwei Filme _____
                                                         (7a)

          um 7 _____.
              (7b)

SCORE [   ]

G. You and a friend want to go out together. Suggest three things you could do. Use different ways of suggesting.
3 points

1. _____

2. _____

3. _____

SCORE [   ]

H. Write a paragraph about your own likes and dislikes. Write at least four complete sentences. You may include:

• what things you do when you go out

• what kinds of movies you like and dislike

• what kinds of music and concerts you like and dislike

• your opinion of particular movies, concerts, stars, or groups

• your favorites
4 points

_____

_____

_____

_____

_____

_____

_____

SCORE [   ]

PART FOUR   Culture (optional)

Maximum Score: 5 extra points

Circle the letter of the answer that best completes the sentence.
5 points

1. *Jenseits von Afrika* ist ein Film mit dem österreichischen Schauspieler _____.

   a. Klaus Maria Brandauer

   b. Robert Redford

   c. Marlene Dietrich

2. Du kannst Rockkonzerte _____ hören.

   a. im Royal-Filmpalast

   b. in der Alabamahalle

   c. in einem Eiscafé

3. *Das Boot* ist _____.

   a. eine deutsche Komödie

   b. ein deutscher Kriegsfilm

   c. eine deutsche Rockgruppe

4. Amerikanische Filme spielen _____ in Deutschland.

   a. viel

   b. selten

   c. nie

5. Peter Maffay, Herbert Grönemeyer und Nina Hagen sind deutsche _____.

   a. Sportler

   b. Tänzer

   c. Sänger

SCORE _____

UNIT 11 TEST

PART ONE   Listening

Maximum Score: 31 points

A. Some friends are discussing presents to give for various occasions. Listen to what they say. Are they wondering what to give, or are they making suggestions? Place a check mark in the appropriate row.
8 points

	1	2	3	4	5	6	7	8
wondering what to give								
making gift suggestions								

SCORE _____

B. This is a busy month for Monika. Jot down the important dates on her calendar. As she mentions each occasion, jot down a word or two in the appropriate space to remind her.
6 points

JUNI

Mo	Di	Mi	Do	Fr	Sa	So
		1	2	3	4	5
6	7	8	9	10	11	12
13	14	15	16	17	18	19
20	21	22	23	24	25	26
27	28	29	30			

SCORE _____

C. Andrea and Monika are in a clothing store looking at the items pictured below. Listen to their comments and determine which item they are talking about. Write the *color* they would like the particular item in below the corresponding picture. You will hear each item twice.

10 points

 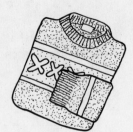   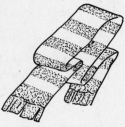

_____ _____ _____ _____ _____

_____ _____ _____ _____ _____

SCORE [   ]

D. Listen to these fragments of conversation overheard in a store. Decide whether the salesclerk's responses are appropriate or not and place a check mark in the appropriate row.

7 points

	1	2	3	4	5	6	7
appropriate							
not appropriate							

SCORE [   ]

PART TWO   Reading

Maximum Score: 21 points

A. You overheard part of these conversations. Complete them with lines taken from the lettered answer choices. For each one, write the letter of your answer choice in the appropriate space in the dialog.
5 points

a. Ich habe ihm eine Platte gekauft.

b. Ich möchte für sie ein Album machen.

c. Ja, wirklich! Das ist ja toll! Was schenkst du ihnen?

d. Was für eine?

e. Was schenkst du ihm?

A: Mein Bruder hat heute Geburtstag.

B: _____
         (1)

A: _____
         (2)

B: _____
         (3)

A: Die Scorpions. Das ist seine Lieblingsgruppe.

A: Meine Grosseltern haben am Sonntag goldene Hochzeit.

B: _____
         (4)

A: _____
         (5)

B: Das ist eine prima Idee!

SCORE [   ]

B. Paula is buying a present, while her friends wait outside and talk. Match the
questions to the answers. Write the letter of the appropriate answer in the space
provided before each question.
8 points

        a. Am 4. Januar.

        b. Gewöhnlich Blumen.

        c. Gute Idee! Das mache ich. Aber was für ein Buch soll ich kaufen?

        d. Hm, du hast vielleicht recht. Aber was soll ich ihr bloss schenken?

        e. Ich hab's! Ich gebe ihr dieses Jahr ein Gartenbuch!

        f. Ihrer Mutter.

        g. Ja, morgen.

        h. Ja, sie hat Blumen gern.

_____ 1. Wem kauft Paula die Pralinen?

_____ 2. Hat sie Geburtstag?

_____ 3. Wann hat deine Mutter Geburtstag?

_____ 4. Was schenkst du ihr?

_____ 5. Schenkst du ihr immer Blumen?

_____ 6. Wie langweilig! Findest du nicht?

_____ 7. Liest sie gern? Kauf ihr doch ein Buch!

_____ 8. Mensch! Das musst du doch wissen! Hast du keine Ideen?

SCORE [ ]

C. The questionnaire below was filled out by some German teenagers. Read the questionnaire and, based on the information in it, determine whether the statements that follow are true or false. Place a check mark in the appropriate column.
8 points

Name	Geburtstag	Party gehabt?	Lieblingsfarbe	Lieblingsgeschenk
Maria	6. März 1975	nein	Rot	Regenmantel
Thomas	28. Juli 1974	ja	Blau	Kamera
Petra	15. Januar 1976	ja	Gelb	Pulli
Ralf	1. Oktober 1970	nein	Grün	Moped

	stimmt	stimmt nicht

1. Ralf ist zu jung für ein Moped.

2. Thomas hat im Sommer Geburtstag.

3. Er hat keine Geburtstagsparty gehabt.

4. Er fotografiert gern, oder vielleicht möchte er es lernen.

5. Es kann sein, dass Marias Regenmantel rot ist.

6. Petra ist 10 Jahre alt.

7. Ihr Geburtstag ist im Januar.

8. Ihre Mutter hat ihr einen gelben Pulli geschenkt, aber Petra mag diese Farbe nicht.

SCORE

Maximum Score: 48 points

A. Here is your gift list. You are telling your friend what you are giving to each person. Write what you say. Use the possessive **mein.**
5 points

> Mutter / Armband
>
> Vater / Krawatte
>
> Grosseltern / Kalender
>
> Brüder / T-Shirts
>
> Klassenkameradin / Poster

1. Ich schenke _____

2. _____

3. _____

4. _____

5. _____

SCORE [   ]

B. You would like to know what these people are giving as presents. Complete the questions by filling in the blanks with forms of **geben** and appropriate possessives.
14 points

You ask these people what they are giving:

1. deine Freundin   Was _____ du _____ Mutter?

2. deine Klassenkameraden Was _____ wir _____ Lehrer?

3. deine Freunde   Was _____ ihr _____ Eltern?

4. deine Lehrerin   Was _____ Sie _____ Vater?

You ask your mother what these people are giving their own friends and relatives:

5. Was _____ Peter _____ Schwester?

6. Was _____ Julia _____ Freundin?

7. Was _____ Herr und Frau Binder _____ Kindern?

SCORE [   ]

C. Your friend is asking you for advice. Make gift suggestions using the personal pronouns **ihm, ihr,** and **ihnen.**
3 points

1. Meine Mutter hat bald Geburtstag.

   _____

2. Meine Eltern haben bald ihren Hochzeitstag.

   _____

3. Es ist bald Vatertag. Was schenke ich meinem Vater?

   _____

SCORE ☐

D. Monika and Andrea are commenting on various articles as they shop in a department store. Complete Monika's comments with appropriate forms of **dies-.** Complete Andrea's responses with appropriate demonstrative pronouns (forms of **der**).
6 points

MONIKA:

ANDREA:

1. _____ T-Shirt ist lustig.
   Ja, wirklich! _____ ist lustig!

2. Schau, _____ Pulli ist schön.
   Ja, _____ ist sehr schön.

3. Und _____ Bluse ist auch schick.
   Hm, _____ ist aber teuer.

4. Was kosten _____ Schuhe?
   Ich glaube, _____ sind im Angebot — 25 Mark.

5. Wie findest du _____ Mantel?
   _____ mag ich nicht so gern.

6. Hm, ich kaufe _____ Hemd in Hellblau.
   Ja, _____ nehme ich auch, aber in Rot.

SCORE ☐

E. Now the girls are asking about prices. Complete the salesclerk's responses by filling in each blank with an appropriate form of **jed-**.
3 points

MÄDCHEN:

VERKÄUFERIN:

1. Was kostet die Mütze?

_____ Mütze kostet 8 Mark.

2. Wie teuer ist der Pulli?

_____ Pulli kostet 18 Mark.

3. Und das Hemd? Auch 18 Mark?

Nein, _____ Hemd kostet nur 12 Mark.

4. Sind die Blusen im Angebot?

Ja, _____ Bluse kostet 14 Mark.

5. Haben Sie dieses T-Shirt in Weiss?

Ja, Sie bekommen _____ T-Shirt in Weiss.

6. Und, bitte, wie teuer ist dieser Mantel?

Sie bekommen _____ Mantel für 60 Mark.

SCORE [____]

F. You are in a store looking at sweaters. Write a conversation that takes place between you and the sales clerk. You get her attention, she responds. You ask how much a sweater costs and whether they have it in green. The sweater is on sale and they do have it in green. You decide to take it.
7 points

DU _____
                              (1)

VERKÄUFERIN _____
                              (2)

DU _____
                              (3)

VERKÄUFERIN _____
                              (4)

DU _____
                              (5)

VERKÄUFERIN _____
                              (6)

DU _____
                              (7)

SCORE [____]

G. You are asking friends what they gave various members of their family as presents. Ask three questions, using the verbs **geben, schenken,** and **kaufen** in the conversational past.
3 points

1. _____

2. _____

3. _____

SCORE [   ]

H. Now a friend asks you when your birthday was, and you answer. Write the exchange in the conversational past.
2 points

FREUND _____
                                    (1)

DU _____
                                    (2)

SCORE [   ]

I. Write how you express good wishes on the following occasions.
5 points

1. dein Freund hat Geburtstag

_____

2. deine Grosseltern haben ihren Hochzeitstag

_____

3. Weihnachten

_____

4. Muttertag

_____

5. Vatertag

_____

SCORE [   ]

PART FOUR   Culture (optional)

Maximum Score: 5 extra points

Read each statement and determine whether it is true or false. Place a check mark in
the appropriate column.
5 points

	stimmt	stimmt nicht

1. In Deutschland gibt es keine Einkaufszentren.

2. Abends und am Wochenende kannst du in Deutschland immer
   einkaufen gehen.

3. Einmal im Monat gibt es in grossen Städten einen langen Samstag.

4. An einem langen Samstag kannst du bis 6 Uhr einkaufen.

5. Wenn man in Deutschland Freunde besucht, bringt man meistens
   etwas Schokolade für die Kinder mit.

SCORE _____

REVIEW TEST 3 • Units 9–12

PART ONE Listening

Maximum Score: 50 points

A. You will hear some young people inviting each other to do various things. Decide whether the person being invited in each mini-dialog accepts or declines the invitation. Place a check mark in the appropriate row.
12 points

	1	2	3	4	5	6
accept						
decline						

SCORE

B. A friend of yours is telling you what presents he's giving to various people. Listen to what he says and write the person it is for under the picture of the present. You will hear each item twice.
10 points

_____   _____   _____

_____   _____   _____

SCORE

C. Listen to the following conversations and decide where they are taking place. Place a check mark in the appropriate row.
10 points

	1	2	3	4	5
bei der Geburtstagsparty					
im Kaufhaus					
im Kino					
im Konzert					
im Restaurant					

SCORE

D. These young people are talking about what they did yesterday. You didn't quite catch the end of what they were saying, but you can figure it out. For each one, write the number of the sentence in front of the past participle that best completes it.
8 points

_____ besucht   _____ gehabt

_____ geblieben   _____ gelesen

_____ gefahren   _____ gesehen

_____ gegangen   _____ gespielt

SCORE

E. Listen to the following conversations. What is being expressed? A compliment? A suggestion? An opinion? Determine which one it is and place a check mark in the appropriate row.
10 points

	1	2	3	4	5	6	7	8	9	10
compliment										
suggestion										
opinion										

SCORE

PART TWO   Reading

Maximum Score: 30 points

A. Read the advertisement printed below and then answer the questions that follow.
10 points

Vergessen Sie die Mutter nicht!

Bald ist Muttertag!

Und was schenken Sie bloss Ihrer Mutter?

Brauchen Sie eine Idee?

Schenken Sie ihr Pralinen!   **Kaufen Sie ihr Parfüm!**

Geben Sie ihr eine Halskette!   **Bringen Sie ihr Blumen!**

Laden Sie sie zum Essen ein!

Und wo finden Sie das alles? — Bei Oberpollinger, natürlich!

Das Kaufhaus mit Ideen!

Oberpollinger hat's — für den Vater, für die Mutter, für die Kinder

auch mit erstklassigem Restaurant
im Obergeschoss

1. Für wen sollst du ein Geschenk kaufen? _____

2. Warum? _____

3. Was für Geschenkideen findest du in dieser Reklame?

_____

4. Was ist Oberpollinger? _____

5. Kann man auch bei Oberpollinger essen? _____

SCORE [   ]

B. Read the letter below and determine whether the statements that follow are true or not. Place a check mark in the appropriate column.
10 points

München, den 16. Februar

Liebe Tante Anni!

Heute habe ich Geburtstag, und ich möchte Dir ganz herzlich für Deine Karte und das schöne Geschenk danken! Die Bluse ist wirklich toll! Blau ist ja meine Lieblingsfarbe! Sie passt auch ganz prima.

Am Samstag habe ich eine Party gehabt. Ich habe meine Klassenkameraden und auch zwei Lehrer eingeladen. Es hat Spass gemacht! Wir haben viel gegessen — wir haben Bratwurst und Kartoffelsalat gehabt, und Mutti hat wieder einen tollen Kuchen gebacken.

Wann besuchst du uns wieder? Im Sommer vielleicht? Es gibt dann viel zu tun. Wir können ins Konzert gehen. Im Sommer haben sie immer Konzerte im Schlossgarten. Wir können auch wieder einen Stadtbummel in der Innenstadt machen. In der Fussgängerzone ist bei dem warmen Wetter immer viel los! Der Englische Garten ist im Sommer auch besonders schön.

So, Tante Anni, nochmals vielen Dank für Deine guten Wünsche zum Geburtstag und für die hübsche Bluse!

Viele liebe Grüsse
Deine Karin

	stimmt	stimmt nicht
1. Tante Anni wohnt in München.		
2. Karin hat im Sommer Geburtstag.		
3. Tante Anni hat Karin eine Bluse geschenkt.		
4. Karin mag die Farbe Blau.		
5. Karin hat eine Party gehabt.		
6. Sie hat keine Lehrer eingeladen.		
7. Es hat auf Karins Party nichts zu essen gegeben.		
8. Karin sagt, dass Tante Anni im Sommer kommen soll.		
9. Aber Karin weiss nicht, was sie zusammen machen können. Sie hat keine Ideen.		
10. In der Fussgängerzone ist es im Sommer besonders langweilig.		

SCORE

C. Here is Uschi's calendar for July. Refer to the calendar to answer the questions that follow.
10 points

JULI					
Sonntag	27	4	11	18 *Stadtfest*	25
Montag	28	5	12 *Tenniskurs*	19	26
Dienstag	29 *Geburtstagsparty für Sabine*	6	13	20 *Vatis Geburtstag*	27 *Rockkonzert*
Mittwoch	30	7	14	21	28
Donnerstag	1 *Kino!*	8	15 *grosseltern kommen*	22	29 *Ferien mit Eltern*
Freitag	2	9	16	23	30
Samstag	3	10 *Fussballspiel aus Mexiko*	17	24 *Sommerfest*	31

1. Wer hat am 20. Juli Geburtstag? _____

2. Wann macht Uschi den Tenniskurs? _____

3. Am 3. Juli möchte Uschis Freund Günther in die Disko gehen. Hat Uschi Zeit?

_____

4. An welchem Tag beginnen die Ferien für Uschi und ihre Familie?

_____

5. Uschis Freundin Natalie fährt am 11. Juli nach Österreich. Kann Uschi auch nach Österreich

fahren? _____

SCORE ☐

A. Karin is having a party. She plans to invite a number of people. Complete the following sentences or questions with appropriate verb forms and pronouns.
12 points

1. Karin soll Klaus und Hans-Peter anrufen. Die Jungen fragen:

    „Karin, wann _____ du _____ _____?"

2. Karin will immer ihre Klassenkameradin Sabine einladen. Sabine fragt:

    „Karin, wann _____ du _____ _____?"

3. Karin hat am Samstag die Party. Sie möchte Sabine einladen. Sie sagt:

    „Sabine, ich habe eine Party, und ich _____ _____ _____."

4. Karin möchte auch ihre Kusinen einladen. Sie sagt:

    „Lisa und Heidi, ich habe eine Party, und ich _____ _____ _____."

5. Was sagt Karin zu ihrem Mathelehrer?

    „Herr Schmidt, ich habe eine Party, und ich möchte _____ _____."

6. Karin fragt Fräulein Seifert und Frau Lange, ob sie am Samstag etwas vorhaben. Karin fragt:

    „_____ Sie am Samstag etwas _____? Ich möchte _____ einladen."

SCORE [   ]

B. Karin's friends are asking about the food at the party. What do they ask? Complete each question by filling in the blank with the appropriate form of **was für ein.**
5 points

DIE GÄSTE:		KARIN:
1. _____ Bowle gibt es?		Eine Erdbeerbowle.
2. _____ Salat machst du?		Einen Kartoffelsalat.
3. _____ Brot soll ich nehmen?		Nimm doch ein Wurstbrot!
4. _____ Kuchen ist das?		Ein Käsekuchen.
5. _____ Würste hast du?		Bratwürste und Weisswürste.

SCORE [   ]

C. Poor Michaela! She has a whole list of things she can't eat and drink. Here is the list: **Pralinen, Kuchen, Eis, Käse, Wurst, Kaffee, Cola und Milch.** Write what she says, using **kein.**
4 points

Ich esse _____

_____

Ich trinke _____

_____

SCORE [   ]

D. Complete the following conversations, which took place at the party. Fill in the first line of each conversation with the correct form of **welch-,** the second with the correct form of **dies-,** and the third with the appropriate demonstrative pronoun.
12 points

1. A: _____ Platte möchtest du hören?

   B: _____ Platte ist gut.

   A: Ja, _____ mag ich auch.

2. A: Du kennst meine Witze alle. _____ Witz soll ich erzählen?

   B: Erzähl mal _____ Witz mit dem Hund!

   A: Ja, _____ ist lustig.

3. A: _____ Ratespiel spielst du gern?

   B: Machen wir _____ Spiel mit Farben.

   A: Ach, _____ finde ich langweilig.

4. A: Karin, du sagst, deine Kusinen kommen auch zur Party. _____ Kusinen sind das? Deine Kusinen aus Berlin?

   B: Nein, _____ Kusinen kommen aus Hamburg.

   A: Ach so, _____ kenne ich nicht.

SCORE [   ]

E. Karin's friends are discussing movies and concerts. Complete the dialogs by filling in each blank with the correct form of **welch-, jed-,** or **was für ein,** choosing whichever is appropriate.
6 points

1. A: _____ Film möchtest du sehen?

   B: Den Film *12 Uhr mittags.*

   A: _____ Film ist das?

   B: Ein Western.

   A: Du willst _____ Western sehen.

   B: Na und? Ich mag Westerns!

2. A: _____ Konzert ist das?

   B: Ein Rockkonzert.

   A: Und _____ Gruppe spielt?

   B: Die Gruppe Queen. Magst du sie?

   A: Ich mag _____ Rockgruppe!

SCORE [ ]

F. Here's what Karin and her friends did last night. Write a paragraph in the conversational past telling what they did:

Karin / in die Stadt fahren

Bernd / Tennis spielen

Brigitte / Freunde besuchen und Platten hören

Heidi und Lisa / zu Hause bleiben

Michaela / ein Buch lesen

Uwe / ins Konzert gehen
7 points

_____

_____

_____

_____

_____

_____

_____

SCORE [ ]

G. Now write a dialog. First ask Brigitte what she did last night, and give her responses; then ask Heidi and Lisa what they did. Heidi answers for both.
10 points

Du   Brigitte, _____
                                                   (1)

Brigitte _____
                                                 (2)

_____
                                                 (3)

Du   Heidi und Lisa, _____
                                                 (4)

Heidi   _____
                                                 (5)

SCORE ☐

H. What are these young people giving as presents? Complete the sentences by filling in each blank with an appropriate possessive or pronoun.
8 points

1. Bernds Vater braucht eine Krawatte. Was schenkt Bernd _____ Vater? Er schenkt

   _____ eine Krawatte.

2. Karins Mutter mag Blumen. Was schenkt Karin _____ Mutter? Sie schenkt

   _____ Blumen!

3. Lisas und Heidis Eltern essen gern Pralinen. Was schenken die Mädchen _____

   Eltern? Sie schenken _____ Pralinen!

4. Karin fragt Lisa und Heidi: „Was schenkt ihr _____ Eltern?" Sie sagen:

   „Wir schenken _____ Eltern Pralinen."

SCORE ☐

I. You and your friends want to go out together. Write three suggestions for things you can do.
3 points

1. _____

2. _____

3. _____

SCORE ☐

J. On Saturday, May 3, it's your birthday. You are having a party. Invite your best friend. He or she accepts.
3 points

Du _____
(1)

_____
(2)

Freund/in _____
(3)

SCORE [ ]

PART FOUR Culture (optional)

Maximum Score: 10 extra points

A. Show how much you know about Germany and other German-speaking countries! Decide which of the lettered answer choices correctly completes each statement. Circle the letter of your choice.
6 points

1. Rotkäppchen ist _____.

   a. eine deutsche Sängerin von Weltrang

   b. ein Märchen

   c. eine Wurstsorte

2. In der Alabamahalle kann man _____.

   a. amerikanische Filme sehen

   b. Rockkonzerte hören

   c. Tennis spielen

3. Klaus Maria Brandauer ist _____.

   a. ein deutscher Rocksänger

   b. ein österreichischer Rocksänger

   c. ein österreichischer Filmstar

4. Fieberbrunn ist _____.

   a. in Tirol

   b. in der Schweiz

   c. in Hessen

5. Eine Tiroler Speckplatte ist etwas _____.

   a. zum Trinken

   b. zum Essen

   c. zum Hören

6. In St. Ulrich kann man _____.

   a. nur schwimmem

   b. nur Schi laufen

   c. schwimmen und Schi laufen

SCORE [ ]

B. Name, in German, three kinds of specialty stores found in Germany and give the typical closing hours for stores in general.
4 points

1. _____

2. _____

3. _____

4. _____

Samstag _____

SCORE [ ]

FINAL TEST • Units 7–12

PART ONE   Listening

Maximum Score: 45 points

A. You and your classmates are sight-seeing in Munich, and you would like to visit some of the famous places you talked about in your German class. Your classmates think they remember where many of the sights are located, but they ask you to check it on the map. Do they remember correctly? Check the map below as you listen to their statements and questions. In each case, decide whether your classmate is right or not. Place a check mark in the appropriate row.
14 points

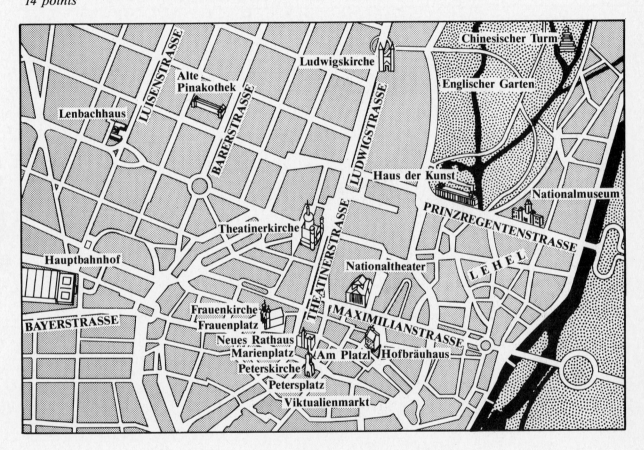

	1	2	3	4	5	6	7
stimmt							
stimmt nicht							

SCORE

B. The young people listed below are discussing what they did yesterday. Listen to their conversation to find out what each of them did. Place a check mark in the appropriate column or columns.
12 points

	Kino	Disko	Konzert	Stadt-bummel	Sport-veranstaltung	zu Hause bleiben
Jens						
Jörg						
Mona						
Kristin						
Lars						

SCORE [ ]

C. What are these young people talking about? Listen to each conversation and decide what the gist of the conversation is. Circle the letter of the statement that most accurately describes what the conversation is about.
9 points

1. a. planning a party

   b. looking for clothes in a department store

   c. buying a birthday present

2. a. discussing what to do when you go out

   b. discussing what to do at a party

   c. discussing your day at school

3. a. deciding what to eat in a restaurant

   b. shopping for groceries

   c. planning food for a party

SCORE [ ]

D. Look at the pictures below as you listen to some descriptions of situations. For each one, decide which picture corresponds to the description and write the number of the description below that picture.
10 points

_____   _____   _____

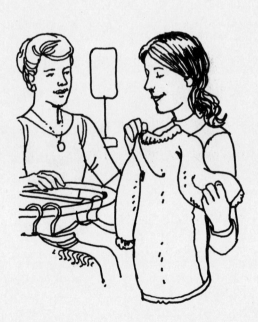

_____   _____

SCORE [   ]

A. Here are some excerpts and ads from German magazines and newspapers. Look at each one and the incomplete statement or statements that follow. Decide which of the lettered answer choices best completes each statement, and circle the letter of that answer.
30 points

Der neue *Passat* ist da.

Fahren in einer neuen Dimension.

Fahrkomfort, Raumkomfort, Styling, Preis.

Nicht nur für eine neue *Generation*, sondern eine neue *Dimension* im Automobilbau.

---

1. This is an ad for a new _____.

   a. home   b. car   c. bicycle

Reisewetterbericht vom 14. April
Vorhersage für Freitag bis Sonntag

Norddeutschland: Sonnig, am Sonntag im Westen stärkere Bewölkung, Regen. Kalt und windig. Anfangs zwischen 8 und 12 Grad, später 12 bis 14 Grad.

Süddeutschland: Nachmittags bewölkt, am Wochenende meist sonnig. Höchsttemperaturen um 15 Grad bis um 20 Grad.

Österreich/Schweiz: Heiter bis wolkig, am Sonntag Regen, in den Bergen Schnee, später Schauer.

---

2. You would like to take a weekend trip. You would have the best weather in _____.

   a. northern Germany   b. southern Germany   c. Austria and Switzerland

3. This is a weather report for a weekend in _____.

   a. summer   b. fall   c. spring

Hier ist der Kaufhof — Sie haben gewonnen!

Ein Gewinnspiel für alle, die ein Telefon haben.

Sie können gewinnen, wenn die letzten 3 Zahlen Ihrer privaten Telefonnummer in diesen Glückszahlen enthalten sind!

2 7 0 8 1 6 4 9 1

4. This ad _____.

   a. invites you to participate in a contest   b. tells you that you have won a new telephone
   c. asks you to call the number shown in order to win a prize

(continued on next page)

**Telefonieren ins Ausland ist billiger, als Sie denken.
3 Minuten USA nur 11,04 DM.**

Ruf doch mal an!  **POST**

5. This ad is encouraging you to _____.

   a. write someone in the United States   b. call someone in the United States

   c. visit someone in the United States

ROT
KOMMT GUT!

*Eine tolle Farbe, die echt Power in
den Frühling '88 bringt. Bei Shirts
und Schuhen, Hosen, Kleidern und
Minis — überall dominiert jetzt die Farbe der Liebe.
Und auch Accessoires kommen besonders gut in Rot.*

6. You would probably read this ad in a _____.

   a. sports magazine   b. news magazine   c. fashion magazine

7. The main idea of this ad is that _____.

   a. red is the color this spring   b. the color red is too domineering

   c. you should buy a ski outfit in red

(continued on next page)

8. In this ad the efficiency of the Zurich airport is compared to that of a _____.

   a. spaceship

   b. car

   c. train station

   d. watch

9. You would be interested in this ad if you wanted to _____.

   a. take a camping vacation

   b. learn a language

   c. improve your grade in math

10. This organization is located in _____.

   a. Switzerland

   b. Austria

   c. Germany

SCORE

B. Renate Jäger has just received a letter from her friend Karin Haupt. Read the letter and determine whether the statements that follow are true or not. Place a check mark in the appropriate column.
24 points

München, den 30. Mai 1989

Liebe Renate!

Bald haben wir Ferien. Warum besuchst Du uns nicht in München? Wir haben Dich lange nicht mehr gesehen, und im Sommer gibt es besonders viel zu tun. Wir können ins Kino und ins Theater gehen. Im Schlossgarten gibt es immer schöne Konzerte. Wir können Stadtbummel durch die Innenstadt machen und dann auch einkaufen gehen. In der Fussgängerzone ist immer viel los. Wir können im Freien sitzen, ein Eis essen und uns die Leute ansehen!

Meine Schwester kommt im Juni zurück. Sie ist ein Jahr in Amerika gewesen. Sie ist dort in die Schule gegangen und hat ein tolles Jahr gehabt. Sie kann uns dann alles erzählen. Vielleicht können wir das auch mal machen!

Hoffentlich sehen wir Dich im Sommer! Schreib bald!

Viele Grüsse

Deine Karin

	stimmt	stimmt nicht
1. Renate wohnt in München.		
2. Sie soll Karin besuchen.		
3. Renate kommt jedes Wochenende nach München.		
4. Karin geht nicht gern aus. Sie bleibt am liebsten zu Hause.		
5. Karins Schwester ist in Amerika und kommt bald nach Hause.		
6. Sie ist eine Schülerin.		
7. Sie mag Amerika nicht.		
8. Karin möchte auch mal nach Amerika reisen.		

SCORE [ ]

FINAL TEST **203**

C. Here is a page from Michael's weekly calendar. Take a look at the activities he has planned for the week and read the statements that follow. Determine whether the statements are true or not and place a check mark in the appropriate column.
21 points

27. Woche Montag **29**	Dienstag **30**	Mittwoch **1**	Donnerstag **2**	Freitag **3**	Samstag **4**
8 *1. Ferientag!*					8
9					10 *Hamburg –*
10				*Omas*	12 *Onkel Heinz*
11				*Geburtstag*	14
12			*Stadtbummel*		
13 *Gartenparty*		*Windsurfing–*	*mit Antje*		Sonntag **5**
14 *bei Stefan*		*kurs*	*(Geschenk*		
15			*f. Oma kaufen)*		16
16					18
17	*Tennis*				20
18					
19					
20 **Juni/Juli**	*Falco-Konzert*			*Disko*	

	stimmt	stimmt nicht
1. Michael hat diese Woche jeden Tag Schule.		
2. Am Mittwoch geht er ins Kino.		
3. Er möchte Windsurfen lernen.		
4. Am Wochenende besucht Michael seinen Onkel in Hamburg.		
5. Michael spielt nie Tennis.		
6. Am Freitag hat Michaels Grossmutter Geburtstag.		
7. Michael soll am 2. Juli mit Stefan einkaufen gehen. Sie wollen alles für die Party holen.		

SCORE [   ]

PART THREE   Writing

Maximum Score: 80 points

A. Wiebke has her week all planned. The paragraph that follows tells you what her plans
are for each day. Now imagine that it's the end of the week and you're Wiebke,
telling what you did during the week just past. Write what you would say, using the
ich-form in the conversational past. Make all necessary changes.
20 points

Am Montag fährt sie mit Karin in die Stadt. Sie machen einen Stadtbummel, und
dann gehen sie in ein Café und essen ein Eis. Am Dienstag bleibt sie zu Hause. Am
Mittwoch besucht sie ihre Grossmutter. Sie spielen Karten und trinken zusammen
Kaffee. Wiebke geht am Donnerstag ins Kino. Sie sieht den Film *Jenseits von Afrika*.
Freitag hat ihre Mutter Geburtstag. Wiebke kauft ihrer Mutter ein Geschenk. Was
gibt Wiebke ihrer Mutter? Eine Halskette. Wiebkes Geschwister sind alle zu Hause.
Sie haben eine kleine Party.

_____

_____

_____

_____

_____

_____

_____

_____

_____

SCORE [   ]

HBJ material copyrighted under notice appearing earlier in this work.

FINAL TEST   **205**

B. Write a short letter to a friend, inviting him or her to a party you are having. Mention who else is coming and what you are having to eat and drink. Ask your friend to bring his or her music cassettes. *10 points*

_____, den _____. Juni 19_____

Liebe (r) _____!

_____

_____

_____

_____

_____

_____

_____

Ich hoffe, du kannst kommen!

Viele Grüsse

Dein(e) _____

SCORE [   ]

C. Write what you would say in the following situations.
30 points

1. You are in the city of Munich and don't know your way around.

   a. Ask a policeman for directions to the **Nationalmuseum.**

   _____.

   b. Someone asks you where the **Marienplatz** is; say you don't know.

   _____.

2. Your sister is going downtown.

   a. Ask her to buy a paper.

   _____.

   b. Tell her to go by bus.

   _____.

(continued on next page)

3. Your friend is having a party and invites you.

   a. Say you can't come; give a reason.

   _____.

   b. Say that you're sorry you can't make it.

   _____.

4. Another friend is having a party. This time you are able to come.

   a. Accept the invitation.

   _____.

   b. At the party, your friend asks you how you like the food; you answer.

   _____.

   c. Compliment your friend's mother on the delicious cake.

   _____.

5. You and your friend want to go out together, and you are discussing what to do.

   a. Suggest going to the movies.

   _____.

   b. One of your friends suggests a western. Say you don't like westerns.

   _____.

   c. Say you like comedies best.

   _____.

   d. Say you don't care one way or the other.

   _____.

(continued on next page)

6. Express good wishes on the following occasions:

   a. Your friend's birthday

   _____ .

   b. Your parents' anniversary

   _____ .

   c. Father's Day

   _____ .

   d. Christmas

   _____ .

   SCORE [＿＿＿＿]

D. You would like to spend a year in Germany, Austria, or Switzerland as an exchange student. An organization that arranges such exchanges has asked you to write a paragraph about yourself. Write the paragraph, including the following information:

   • name, age, where you are from
   • name of school, favorite subjects
   • sports, hobbies, activities
   • some of your favorite books, authors, film stars, singers, or groups

20 points

   _____

   _____

   _____

   _____

   _____

   _____

   _____

   _____

   _____

   SCORE [＿＿＿＿]

PART FOUR Culture (optional)

Maximum Score: 40 extra points

A. Can you name the eleven German states, the **Bundesländer?** List them below.
22 points

1. _____

2. _____

3. _____

4. _____

5. _____

6. _____

7. _____

8. _____

9. _____

10. _____

11. _____

SCORE [   ]

B. Do you know the capital cities of the German-speaking countries? Complete the sentences below by filling in each blank with the name of the correct capital.
10 points

1. The capital of the BRD is _____.

2. The capital of the DDR is _____.

3. The capital of Austria is _____.

4. The capital of Switzerland is _____.

5. The capital of Liechtenstein is _____.

SCORE [   ]

(Part Four continues on page 214)

C. Circle the appropriate completion to each of the following statements.
8 points

1. The capital city of Bavaria, known as the **Weltstadt mit Herz,** is _____.

   a. Hamburg

   b. Frankfurt

   c. Munich

2. A specialty of Munich is _____.

   a. Leberkäs

   b. Hamburger

   c. Fischbrot

3. **Der lange Samstag** refers to the one Saturday a month in Germany when _____.

   a. stores are open until 6

   b. stores are open

   c. stores are closed

4. When you are invited to someone's house in Germany, you would probably _____.

   a. not bring anything

   b. suggest going out to dinner

   c. bring flowers or a box of candy

SCORE [   ]

PROFICIENCY–BASED TEST 1
Practice Test (after Unit 6)

PART ONE   Speaking

The first part of this test is designed to find out how well you speak German. Even though you may not know all the words that you feel you need, make yourself understood as best you can.

A. You're going to hear fifteen questions. Answer them as completely as you can in German.

B. Describe your school day. Say how you get to school, what subjects you have, which ones you do well in, and which ones you find difficult. Mention at what time school begins and when it ends. Also tell something about your after-school activities.

C. Act out the following situations.

1. You're at a party. You introduce yourself to a German person you'd like to know better. Tell that person as many interesting things about yourself as you can.

2. School is finally out for the summer. You're excited about your vacation plans! Tell your German friend about your plans for the first week of vacation.

3. You're going to interview Stefan, a German exchange student, for your school newspaper. Prepare for the interview with Stefan by practicing at least five questions to ask him in German.

4. You're working in the school store. I come to buy something. Greet me and find out what I want. Try to sell me something that I didn't request. Tell me how much money I owe and then say goodbye. I'll act out the situation with you.

PART TWO Listening

The second part of this test is designed to find out how well you understand German. Even though you may not recognize all the words that you hear, listen for the general idea and important details.

A. You're waiting for friends at the airport in Frankfurt and happen to be standing near the monitor. Different people ask you questions. Listen to the questions and help each person find the information on the monitor you see below. Write the information requested in the space provided below the monitor. You will hear each question twice.

Abflug			
Flug Nr.	nach	Zeit	Ausgang
Pan Am 400	Berlin	12.45	B13
Lufthansa 92	Düsseldorf	13.05	B20
Lufthansa 75	München	14.00	B2
Brit. Air 25	London	14.20	A14
Lufthansa 146	Köln	15.00	B10

Ankunft				
Flug Nr.	aus	Zeit		Ausgang
Brit. Air 35	London	13.05	gelandet	B2
Pan Am 80	Boston	13.10	gelandet	A9
Lufthansa 110	Rom	14.15		B3
Lufthansa 600	Paris	14.30		A15
Swiss Air 21	Zürich	15.10		B8

1. _____   4. _____

2. _____   5. _____

3. _____   6. _____

B. You're going to hear a conversation between a sales clerk and a customer in a stationery store. As you listen, look at the picture below and circle the items that the customer decides to buy. Then write the total amount of the sale on the sales receipt. You will hear the conversation twice.

Buchhandlung am Markt	
Artikel	**Preis**
Summe	

C. You're picking out posters to give to various people. Listen to the following conversation about their favorite activities and classes. Then, based on their interests, show which two posters you would pick out for each person. Write the person's name in the space provided below each of the appropriate posters. The names are listed for you as a reminder.

Antje   Jens   Michael   Natalie   Frau Meier

1. _____

2. _____

3. _____

4. _____

5. _____

6. _____

7. _____

8. _____

9. _____

10. _____

PART THREE Reading

The third part of this test is designed to find out how well you read German. Even though you may not recognize all the words that you see, read for the general idea and important details.

A. You've just received letters from two new German-speaking pen pals. Read the letters below and then complete the sentences following them in English.

Zürich, den 5. März

Gruetzi!

Ich heisse Roger Leitner. Ich bin Schweizer, aus Zürich. Ich bin fünfzehn Jahre alt, mache gern Sport und habe auch Hobbys. Ich sammle Briefmarken und Comics-Hefte. In die Schule gehe ich nicht so gern, aber meine Noten sind nicht schlecht. Am liebsten mag ich Mathe — mein Mathematiklehrer ist prima! In Geschichte bin ich schlecht.

Was machst Du am liebsten? Hast Du Hobbys? Bist Du gut in der Schule?

Viele Grüsse
Roger Leitner

Wien, den 20. April

Grüss Dich!

Ich heisse Natalie Sänger. Ich bin vierzehn und bin aus Wien. Ich habe viele Hobbys und Interessen. Ich schwimme, und ich laufe Schi. Spiele wie Schach und Mau-Mau finde ich blöd. Meine Hobbys sind Münzensammeln und Musik. Ich spiele Gitarre und bin in einer kleinen Rockgruppe. Das macht Spass!

Die Schule ist gut. Wir haben nette Lehrer, und viele Fächer sind interessant. Ich lerne Sprachen gern — am liebsten Englisch und Französisch. Vielleicht mache ich mal eine Reise nach Amerika!

Viele Grüsse
Natalie Sänger

(continued on next page)

1. The boy's name is _____.

2. The girl's name is _____.

3. He is from _____.

4. She is from _____.

5. He likes _____

_____.

6. She likes _____

_____.

7. He doesn't like _____.

8. She doesn't like _____.

B. Read the article below. Answer the questions that follow in German.

Die Schülerin Marianne Neubach wohnt mit ihren Eltern und Geschwistern in einer Wohnung in Köln. Ihr Bruder heisst Markus; er ist zehn Jahre alt. Ihre Schwester, die Antje, ist zwölf. Marianne und ihre Schwester hören gern Musik, schwimmen viel und spielen zweimal in der Woche Tennis. Der Markus macht nicht gern Sport. Er liest lieber und sammelt gern Briefmarken, Münzen, Postkarten — alles!
Die Wohnung von Neubachs ist gross und schön. Sie haben sechs Zimmer. Die Freunde kommen alle gern zu Neubachs. Dort ist es immer nett und gemütlich.

1. Wie heisst Mariannes Schwester? _____

2. Wie alt ist Markus? _____

3. Wer macht gern Sport? _____

4. Wer sammelt gern? _____

5. Wieviel Zimmer hat die Wohnung von Neubachs? _____

PART FOUR   Writing

The fourth part of this test is designed to find out how well you write in German. Even though you may not know all the words that you feel you need, make yourself understood as best you can. Minor errors in spelling and punctuation will be excused in this part of the test.

A. You're thinking about your class schedule for next year. Write five subjects you will probably take.

_____

_____

B. You have to shop for school supplies. Write down five items you will need to buy.

_____

_____

C. Write down five activities you like to do alone or with friends.

_____

_____

D. You are getting ready for a trip to Germany. Write down five items you'll need to take with you.

_____

_____

E. You're at the airport. Write three questions you ask to find your way around.

_____

_____

_____

F. Your teacher has found a German pen pal for you. Write a short note to introduce yourself. Be sure to include details about school, your leisure activities, and your family.

_____

_____

_____

_____

_____

PROFICIENCY–BASED TEST 2
Practice Test (after Unit 12)

PART ONE Speaking

The first part of this test is designed to find out how well you speak German. Even though you may not know all the words that you feel you need, make yourself understood as best you can.

A. You're going to hear ten questions. Answer them as completely as you can in German.

B. Act out the following situations.

1. You're shopping for holiday gifts with your friend and discussing what you plan to buy. Name three people on your gift list and tell what you plan to buy for them.

2. You've invited two friends to your home for the first time. Before they arrive, describe them to your family and tell something about them. For example, you might mention their sports and hobbies.

3. You and your friend Lisa are at a restaurant. Say what you are going to have to eat and to drink, and recommend something to her.

4. You and a friend want to go out together. Make three suggestions for what you can do. Say what you would prefer to do and what you would prefer not to do.

5. After arriving at the airport in Frankfurt, you go to claim your backpack but can't find it. Tell the baggage claim attendant the following:

- what the problem is
- which flight you came in on (the flight number and place of departure)
- details to help identify your backpack (color, size, contents)
- the address and phone number where you're staying

   I'll play the role of the baggage claim attendant.

PART TWO Listening

The second part of this test is designed to find out how well you understand German. Even though you may not recognize all the words that you hear, listen for the general idea and important details.

A. Your German friends are inviting you to do various things with them. As you listen to the six phone messages that they've left on your answering machine, look at the calendar page below. For each invitation, find the appropriate day on the calendar. Fill in the activity, the time, and the name of the person who invited you. You will hear each invitation twice.

Montag	
Dienstag	
Mittwoch	
Donnerstag	
Freitag	
Samstag	
Sonntag	

B. You're going to hear a conversation that takes place in a restaurant. Elke and Jörg are deciding what to have. Before you listen to the conversation, take a minute to look at the incomplete statements below and their suggested completions.

Now listen to the conversation. Then read each incomplete statement again and circle the letter of the best completion. You will hear the conversation twice.

1. Jörg isst _____.

   a. einen Hamburger

   b. eine Bratwurst

   c. Leberkäs mit Senf

2. Elke isst _____.

   a. einen Hamburger

   b. eine Bratwurst

   c. Leberkäs mit Senf

3. Elke trinkt _____.

   a. Cola

   b. Mineralwasser

   c. Milch

4. Jörg hat nicht viel _____.

   a. Hunger

   b. Geld

   c. Senf

5. Um fünf Uhr beginnt _____.

   a. das Essen

   b. das Fussballspiel

   c. die Schule

C. You are sightseeing in Germany and overhear some conversations in which people ask directions to various places. Look at the street map below as you listen to each conversation. Circle the place the first speaker is looking for and determine whether the second speaker's directions are correct or not. Then place a check mark in the appropriate row of boxes below the map. Take a minute now to look at the map.

Now listen to the conversations. You will hear each conversation twice.

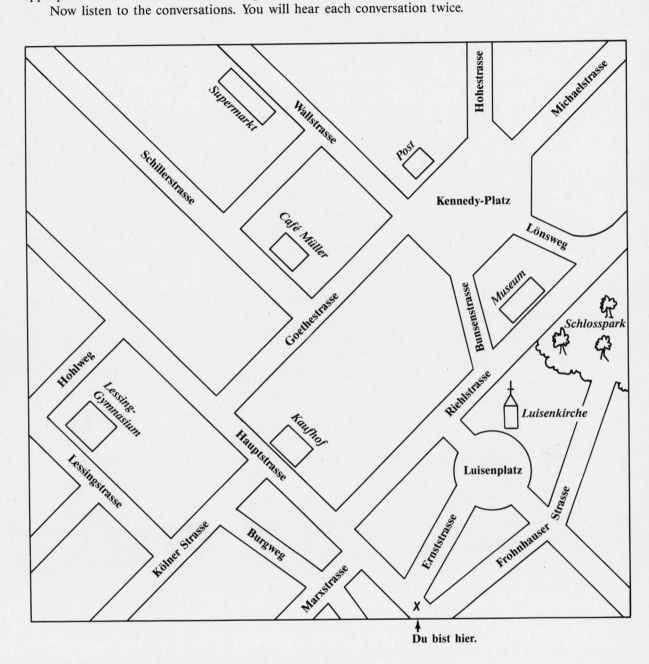

Du bist hier.

	1	2	3	4	5	6
stimmt						
stimmt nicht						

PART THREE Reading

The third part of this test is designed to find out how well you read German. Even though you may not recognize all the words that you see, read for the general idea and important details.

A. You want to have a party. Pick a date and a time for your party and fill in the invitation below to send to your friends.

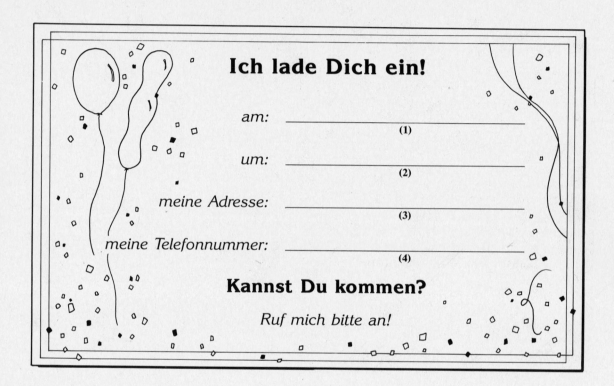

Ich lade Dich ein!

am: _____
(1)

um: _____
(2)

meine Adresse: _____
(3)

meine Telefonnummer: _____
(4)

Kannst Du kommen?

Ruf mich bitte an!

B. Martina Kraft has been keeping a diary. Here is the text of her entry for July 10. Read what she has written and determine whether the statements that follow are true or not. Place a check mark in the appropriate column.

10. Juli

Morgen kommt endlich mein Gast aus Amerika! Greg Miller aus New York! Hoffentlich hat er Köln gern! Na ja, in New York haben sie den Hudson und das Empire State Building, aber dafür haben wir den Rhein und den Dom, und der Kölner Dom ist sechshundert Jahre alt! Und gotisch! Aber vielleicht findet Greg Kirchen langweilig. Dann gehen wir einfach ins Museum. Er schreibt, dass er Musik gern hat. Da gehen wir gleich am Sonntag in ein Konzert! Am Samstag machen wir eine Party. Meine Freunde kennen Greg auch — natürlich nur von Fotos. Sie finden es interessant, dass ich einen amerikanischen Brieffreund habe. Und Deutsch spricht er auch! Nur die Antje findet, dass er arrogant aussieht, aber ich finde ihn sehr sympathisch. Er ist nicht sehr gross, blond, trägt eine Brille und sieht sehr intelligent aus. Antjes Freund Jochen ist ja gross und dunkel und so langweilig! Aber Jungen sind eben Geschmackssache!

	stimmt	stimmt nicht
1. Greg Miller is Martina's pen pal.		
2. Martina lives in Cologne.		
3. The Cologne Cathedral is a modern church.		
4. New York is on the Hudson; Cologne is not located on a river.		
5. Martina is going to take Greg to a concert.		
6. Greg doesn't speak a foreign language.		
7. Martina's friends have all met Greg before.		
8. Greg wears glasses.		
9. Martina doesn't think much of Antje's boyfriend.		
10. Greg will arrive on July 12.		

C. Here is a movie listing from a German newspaper. Look over the movies that are
playing and answer the questions below.

Royal-Filmpalast Kino A	13.00 15.00 17.00	**Feivel- Der Mauswanderer** Eine tapfere Maus gewinnt alle Herzen!	ab 6 Jahre
Royal-Filmpalast Kino B	16.10 18.20 20.30	James-Bond-Festival: Sean Connery **GOLDFINGER** und nächste Woche: **FEUERBALL**	ab 12 Jahre
Royal-Filmpalast Kino C	17.00 19.00 21.00	Die Tanz-Sensation aus den USA! **DIRTY DANCING**	ab 12 Jahre
Sonnen Filmtheater	12.00 14.00 18.15	**Schrei nach Freiheit** Eine wahre Geschichte aus Südafrika	ab 12 Jahre
Stachus-Kino-Center Kino 1	13.50 15.40 17.30	Die einmalige Cher ist **Mondsüchtig** Ein toller Film! Cher gewinnt für ihre Rolle den Oscar!	ab 12 Jahre
Stachus-Kino-Center Kino 2	13.50 15.50 17.50	In den USA sprechen alle von **Wall Street** Die spannende Geschichte von Geiz, Geld und Macht!	ab 12 Jahre

1. In welchem Theater gibt es ein James-Bond-Festival? _____

2. Du findest Tanzen toll. Welchen Film möchtest du sehen? _____

3. Du möchtest mit deinem kleinen Bruder ins Kino gehen. Er ist acht Jahre alt. In welchen Film

   geht ihr? _____

4. Du möchtest den Film *Wall Street* sehen. Wann fängt er an? _____

5. Du interessierst dich für Politik und für andere Länder. Welchen Film willst du sehen?

   _____

6. In welchem Film spielt eine Schauspielerin, die einen Oscar für ihre Rolle gewonnen hat?

   _____

PART FOUR   Writing

The fourth part of this test is designed to find out how well you write German. Even though you may not know all the words that you feel you need, make yourself understood as best you can. Minor errors in spelling and punctuation will be excused in this part of the test.

A. Your family is planning to sell your house. Write an ad for the newspaper. In the ad, do the following:
  - tell how many rooms you have
  - list the rooms
  - at the end, give a few adjectives and details to make the house sound appealing

_____

_____

_____

_____

_____

_____

B. Your father is returning from a business trip earlier than expected. He calls and asks you to pick him up at the airport. You can't go because you have a commitment at school. Your mother should be back shortly. Leave a note for her. In the note, do the following:
  - tell her about your father's arrival
  - give the name of the airport, name of the airline, flight number, and arrival time
  - ask her to pick him up

_____

_____

_____

_____

_____

_____

_____

C. You are having a party. Write a note to a friend inviting him or her. In the note, cover these points:
  - give the date and time of the party
  - mention who else is coming
  - tell what you're having to eat and drink
  - tell some of the things you plan to do at the party

(continued on following page)

PROFICIENCY–BASED TEST 2   **223**

_____

_____

_____

_____

_____

_____

D. Your friend Ulrike has agreed to help you do some errands in preparation for the party. Write a note to Ulrike. In the note, include the following:
- a list of things you need
- advice on where to buy each item

_____

_____

_____

_____

_____

_____

E. You have been corresponding with a German student this year, and your pen pal is coming to visit you during the summer vacation. Write a letter to your pen pal, in which you cover the following points:
- a few things you want to show him or her in your area
- some things you can do together

_____

_____

_____

_____

_____

_____

PROFICIENCY–BASED TEST 3
(after Unit 12)

PART ONE   Speaking

The first part of this test is designed to find out how well you speak German. Even though you may not know all the words that you feel you need, make yourself understood as best you can.

A. You're going to hear fifteen questions. Answer them as completely as you can in German.

B. Act out the following situations.

1. You're ordering a meal in a German restaurant. You're very hungry. The waiter comes to take your order. **Was möchten Sie, bitte?**

2. You are planning a party. Tell your best friend about it. Invite him or her, giving the date and time. Mention who else is coming and what you're having to eat and drink; also mention some of the things you plan to do at the party.

3. You are visiting Germany, and some German students are asking you about school in the United States. What would you tell them? Mention some of the differences between German and American schools; for example, the grading system.

4. You agreed to help me after school, but you found out that you won't be able to. Explain to me why you can't stay (choose any appropriate reason). Then let's make alternate arrangements.

5. On your last report card, all your grades were good except for the one in math. Explain your grade to your parents.

PART TWO Listening

The second part of this test is designed to find out how well you understand German. Even though you may not recognize all the words that you hear, listen for the general idea and important details.

A. You're going to hear six radio announcements. Before you listen to the first announcement, take a minute to read the incomplete sentence below and its suggested completions.

     Now listen to the first announcement. Then choose the best completion for the sentence and circle the corresponding letter.

1. Das ist eine Ansage für _____.

   a. eine Sportveranstaltung   c. Filme

   b. ein Konzert   d. ein Restaurant

Before you listen to the second announcement, take a minute to read sentences 2, 3, and 4 and their suggested completions.

     Now listen to the announcement. Then, for each sentence, choose the best completion and circle the corresponding letter.

2. Diese Ansage ist für Leute, die _____ besuchen wollen.

   a. die USA   c. Japan

   b. Frankreich   d. England

3. Du machst diese Reise _____.

   a. mit der Bahn   c. mit dem Schiff

   b. mit dem Flugzeug   d. mit dem Bus

4. Das Reisebüro heisst _____.

   a. Lufthansa   c. Schmidt

   b. Frankfurt   d. Müller

Before you listen to the next announcement, take a minute to read sentences 5, 6, and 7 and their suggested completions.

     Now listen to the announcement. Then, for each sentence, choose the best completion and circle the corresponding letter.

5. Diese Ansage ist für _____.

   a. ein Konzert   c. eine Sportveranstaltung

   b. einen Film   d. eine Geburtstagsparty

6. Die Berliner Philharmoniker ist _____.

   a. eine Rockgruppe   c. ein Orchester

   b. ein Kaufhaus   d. eine Musikschule

7. Herbert von Karajan wird _____.

   a. 20 Jahre alt   c. 50 Jahre alt

   b. 30 Jahre alt   d. 80 Jahre alt   *(continued on next page)*

Before you listen to the fourth announcement, take a minute to read sentences 8, 9, and 10 and their suggested completions.

   Now listen to the announcement. Then, for each sentence, choose the best completion and circle the corresponding letter.

   8. Die Internationale Schule ist eine _____.

      a. Tennisschule   c. Sprachschule

      b. Musikschule   d. Tanzschule

   9. Die Kurse sind _____.

      a. am Morgen und am Nachmittag   c. am Sonntag

      b. am Abend und am Samstag   d. an Weihnachten

  10. Wenn du mehr über der Schule wissen willst, sollst du _____.

      a. anrufen   c. in die Schule kommen

      b. schreiben   d. bei der Post fragen

Before you listen to the fifth announcement, take a minute to read sentences 11 and 12 and their suggested completions.

   Now listen to the announcement. Then, for each sentence, choose the best completion and circle the corresponding letter.

  11. In diesem Geschäft kannst du _____ kaufen.

      a. einen Kuli   c. ein Pfund Hackfleisch

      b. einen Pullover   d. einen Strauss Blumen

  12. Du kannst in diesem Geschäft _____ einkaufen.

      a. am Sonntag   c. von Montag bis Freitag

      b. von Montag bis Samstag   d. nur am Wochenende

Before you listen to the last announcement, take a minute to read sentences 13 and 14 and their suggested completions.

   Now listen to the announcement. Then, for each sentence, choose the best completion and circle the corresponding letter.

  13. Der Adler ist _____.

      a. ein Kaufhaus   c. eine Disko

      b. ein Theater   d. ein Restaurant

  14. Hier kannst du _____.

      a. nur Kaffee trinken   c. gut und preiswert essen

      b. nur gut und teuer essen   d. keinen Hamburger bekommen

B. You're going to hear a taped radio broadcast about two news items. Before you listen to the broadcast, take a minute to read the incomplete sentences below.

　　　Now listen to the radio broadcast. Then complete the sentences below in English. You will hear the broadcast twice.

1. The catastrophe being reported is a _____.

2. The city affected is _____.

3. Erding and Freising are villages near the city of _____.

4. The people are protesting against the construction of a new _____.

C. You are now going to hear a conversation. Before you listen to it, take a minute to read the incomplete sentences below and their suggested completions.

　　　Now listen to the conversation. Then, for each incomplete sentence, choose the best completion and circle the corresponding letter.

1. Die junge Amerikanerin ist _____.

   a. auf der Post

   b. auf der Bank

   c. im Supermarkt

2. Sie hat Deutsch in der Schule gelernt und auch _____.

   a. von ihren Eltern

   b. von ihrer Grossmutter

   c. von ihrem Freund

3. Sie kommt aus _____.

   a. einer Grossstadt

   b. einem Vorort von Washington

   c. einem Dorf

4. Sie ist jetzt in der Stadt _____.

   a. München

   b. Düsseldorf

   c. Dresden

5. Sie möchte wissen, wo sie _____ finden kann.

   a. eine Bank

   b. einen Geschenkladen

   c. ein Telefon

PART THREE Reading

The third part of this test is designed to find out how well you read German. Even though you may not recognize all the words that you see, read for the general idea and important details.

A. Your pen pal, Markus, has volunteered to host students from your school's German exchange program. You offer to fill out the application form for him. You go back to the first letter he sent you to get the information you need. Read his letter (below) and then fill out the application form that follows.

> Bonn, den 8. Dezember
>
> Grüss Dich!
>
> Ich heisse Markus Lender. Ich bin 14 Jahre alt. Ich gehe aufs Gymnasium, in die 9. Klasse. Ich wohne in Bonn, in der Hauptstadt der BRD. Meine Adresse ist Wielandstrasse 9, 53 Bonn. Meine Telefonnummer ist 89 73 40. Ich wohne in einem netten Haus mit meinen Eltern und Geschwistern. Meine Eltern sind beide berufstätig. Meine Mutter heisst Renate. Sie ist Lehrerin für Englisch und Deutsch. Mein Vater heisst Dieter. Er ist Computer-Spezialist. Er arbeitet für eine grosse Firma in Köln. Er fährt jeden Tag mit dem Wagen ins Büro, aber Köln ist nicht sehr weit. Ich habe eine Schwester, die Susanne. Sie ist 16 und geht auch aufs Gymnasium. Mein Bruder heisst Michael. Er ist 8 und geht noch auf die Grundschule. Er macht gern Sport und spielt jeden Tag Fussball. Ich mache auch gern Sport, aber ich kann nicht jeden Tag Fussball spielen! Ich spiele nur einmal in der Woche, am Donnerstag. Wir haben dann Training. Ich spiele auch Tennis und gehe gern schwimmen. Am Wochenende gehe ich oft mit meinen Freunden ins Kino. Am liebsten sehen wir Western und Komödien. Ich höre Musik gern und spiele Gitarre, aber ich kann nicht gut singen!
>
> Viele Grüsse
> Markus

Name _____ Alter _____
          (1)   (2)

Adresse _____
                                     (3)

Telefonnummer _____ Klasse _____
                       (4)   (5)

Sport und Hobbys _____
                                          (6)

Spielen Sie ein Instrument? _____ Was für (ein)? _____
                                 (7)   (8)

Name des Vaters _____ Beruf _____
                             (9)   (10)

Name der Mutter _____ Beruf _____
                             (11)   (12)

Haben Sie Geschwister? _____ Wie viele? _____
                                (13)   (14)

Name(n), Alter _____
                                      (15)

B. You live in Munich and are shopping in a department store. You are looking for a number of things. Where would you find them? Looking at the store directory on the next page, write the floor and the department for each of the following, in German.

1. You have been saving money for a new bike and want to check what this store has.

   _____

2. Your family is planning a trip to France this summer and you want to pick up some brochures.

   _____

3. You need to buy fish food for your tropical fish. _____

   _____

4. Your little sister will be five next week. You want to buy her a present for her birthday.

   _____

5. You need to buy an anniversary card for your grandparents. _____

   _____

6. Your mother has asked you to buy a new bath mat for the upstairs bathroom.

   _____

7. Your father's birthday is coming up. You want to buy him the new best-seller.

   _____

8. Your cousin, who's coming to visit, is something of a gourmet. Where could you get your cousin

   something special to eat? _____

9. On second thought, perhaps you'll take your cousin out to eat. Where could you go?

   _____

(continued on next page)

Das erwartet Sie alles im neuen Haus Niedermeyer am Dom.

4.Etage

Rundfunk/Fernsehen. Weltstadt-Angebote. **HiFi-Studios.** Profi-Sound für alle.

Video-Technik. Ihr Lieblings-programm, wann Sie wollen.

Elektro-Groß- und -Kleingeräte. Komfort einschalten

Restaurant-Café »am Dom«. Spitze! Wie alles bei Niedermeyer am Dom.

Zoo. Das große Herz für Tiere.

3.Etage

Antiquitäten. Bauernmöbel und rustikales Zubehör.

Rahmen-Werkstatt. Ganz neu. Service für den Bilder-Freund.

Geschenkartikel. Unerschöpflich.

Spielwaren. Das Kind ist König.

Glückwunschkarten. Alles zum Schreiben.

Holz- und Bürstenwaren. Das Handlichste und Praktischste.

Kristall und Glas. Berauschend schön.

Porzellan, Steingut, Keramik. Elegant, behaglich, rustikal.

Küchenabteilung. Hinreißend.

2.Etage

Gardinen. Jede Farbe, jedes Dessin. Hier wird die Auswahl zum Vergnügen.

Alles fürs Badezimmer. Die exklusiven Tricks fürs Bad.

Teppiche/Felle. Internationale Kostbarkeiten.

Teppichboden-Studio. Auswahl komplett.

1.Etage

Bürotechnik/Schreibwaren. Vom Mini-Rechner bis zur Super-Schreibmaschine.

Autozubehör. Alles für die Rallye und den Fahrkomfort.

Fahrräder. Von gemütlich bis Rennmaschine.

Motorisierte Zweiräder. Helm auf — zum Vergnügen.

Motorradbekleidung. Bis hin zur teuersten Haut.

Heimwerker. Angebote zum Bauklötze-Staunen.

Erdgeschoß

Foto/Optik. Die ganze weite Foto- und Kamera-Welt.

Sonntagsmalerei. Auch für Montagsmaler.

Augenoptik. Sehschärfe-Test. Brillenberatung durch unseren Augenoptiker-Meister.

Bücherabteilung. 7. Himmel für Bücherwürmer. Über 10 000 Titel!

Zeitungen/Zeitschriften. Druckfrisch aktuell.

Reisebüro »Wanderlust.« Die reine Erholung.

Information. Immer bereit.

Basement

Feinschmecker-Keller. Spezialität Frischware. Frisches Fleisch. Frischer Fisch. Frische Wurst. Frischer Käse. Frisches Brot. Sagenhaft.

Wasch- und Putzmittel. Alles für den gepflegten Haushalt.

Parfümerie »die schöne Helena«. Alles für die Schönheit.

PART FOUR Writing

The fourth part of this test is designed to find out how well you write in German. Even though you may not know all the words that you feel you need, make yourself understood as best you can. Minor errors in spelling and punctuation will be excused in this part of the test.

A. You are planning a trip to Germany this summer. You will be staying with a family with two children — Robert, 12 years old, and Christine, 15. Make a list of at least twelve things you will take along.

_____   _____

_____   _____

_____   _____

_____   _____

_____   _____

_____   _____

B. You have just had a party and are writing a letter to a friend who has moved away and therefore could not come. In the letter, cover the following details:

• when you had the party

• who was there

• what you had to eat and drink

• what you did

_____

_____

_____

_____

_____

_____

_____

_____

C. Your teacher has just given you the name of a prospective pen pal in Germany. Write a letter introducing yourself. Include information about the place you live, your family, your school, your activities, your likes and dislikes, and anything else you find interesting to mention.

_____

_____

_____

_____

_____

_____

_____

_____

_____

_____

D. Write a radio commercial for a store of your choice. In it, mention several items a customer would want to buy there. Be sure to include the following information:

- details about the items (such as price, size, color, and so on)
- location of the store
- days and hours the store is open
- other details that might attract customers

_____

_____

_____

_____

_____

_____

_____

_____

_____

_____

E. You're the movie critic for your school newspaper. Write a review of a movie you saw recently. Be sure to include the following information:

- the title of the movie
- where it's playing
- what type of movie it is
- what you thought of it

_____

_____

_____

_____

_____

_____

_____

_____

_____

_____

C 1
D 2
E 3
F 4
G 5
H 6
I 7
J